Ma

Prov. 3:6

DRIVE-THRU JESUS

MARK MILLER

CROSSBOOKS
PUBLISHING

CrossBooks™
A Division of LifeWay
One LifeWay Plaza
Nashville, TN 37234
www.crossbooks.com
Phone: 1-866-768-9010

First published by CrossBooks 10/27/2014

ISBN: 978-1-4627-5565-3 (sc)
ISBN: 978-1-4627-5564-6 (e)

Library of Congress Control Number: 2014918460

Printed in the United States of America.

This book is printed on acid-free paper.

CONTENTS

This book is dedicated to my wife Carrie for allowing me the time to finish this work. Many of these stories we have experienced together and I thank the Lord for them all. A special thanks is given to my very good friend Keith. We set out together to each write a book and of course yours was completed two years earlier. I also want to say thanks to my friend Jimmy for constantly encouraging me to write and put my words in print. We all need someone to push us along and you served that role well.

DRIVE – THRU JESUS

"Your servant has been keeping his father's sheep. When a lion or a bear came and carried off a sheep from the flock, I went after it, struck it and rescued the sheep from its mouth. When it turned on me, I seized it by its hair, struck it and killed it...The Lord who delivered me from the paw of the lion and the paw of the bear will deliver me from the hand of the Philistine (1 Samuel 17:34 - 37)."

- David, Son of Jesse

God is always preparing you.

You may not realize it at first, but He's working all of your life together for His good. Upon reflection, it may seem obvious. But that's not always the case in the present.

David knew that. I'm not talking about King David, but teen David. Long before David became king of Israel, years before his slip-up with Bathsheba, even before he squared off against mighty Goliath, David was a shepherd. He watched his father's sheep.

Now, you and I might not think that's too great a job, but if your family's livelihood depended on the raising of sheep, I'd say that's quite a compliment to be given such responsibility.

"Here son, take care of our sheep. Travel with them for months. Move them to green pastures. Lead them to still waters. Here's a sword, a sling and your staff. Good luck."

My guess is that initially David had no idea of all God had in store for him. Who really does? I'm sure on occasion he got tired, lonely and even scared. But that's where David grew up. God used these experiences to mature a young man, to prepare him for a life's adventure.

One day, David left the flock to someone else's care and under his father's instructions, went to check on his older brothers. They were in the army, at war against the Philistines.

When teen David arrived on the scene he heard the enemy soldier Goliath, a huge intimidating man, belittling Israel and the Lord. He couldn't believe his ears. He couldn't believe his eyes.

Why isn't anyone doing something here? How can you let this guy go on? He's a disgrace. Somebody do something!

That's when it occurred to David. *That guy looks like a lion. He reminds me of a bear I once met, you know, the one hanging on the wall of my tent back home. God has prepared me for such a time as this.*

So with a sling and stone, he struck Goliath in the head; and then with the giant's own sword, he cut off his head.

The soldiers rallied. The Philistines were routed and God received the glory.

I have never been a shepherd.

We raised cows when I was a kid, but I don't know a thing about sheep. As of this writing, I've never traveled to Israel. But I have had a lot of experiences growing up. And looking back now, I can see how God used many of those experiences to shape me; to prepare me for such a time as this.

Unlike David, I'm not a ruler of nations. But I am a shepherd of sorts. I'm a pastor and from what I remember in Greek class they come from the same root word. David pastored sheep and I pastor people.

None of which likely matters to you. But you have your own experiences, your own job, your own family. And that does matter. It matters because God is taking all your past experiences and working them together for His good in the present.

That's what this book is about.

It's a collection of experiences, some funny, some sad, and the life lessons we can find within. I'm convinced that God is teaching us every day in His ongoing attempt to shape us more and more into the image of His Son.

King David learned from his experiences and defeated an enemy that all others feared. He would later write, upon reflection, Psalm 23:

"The Lord is my shepherd. I shall not want.

He makes me lie down in green pastures.

He leads me beside quiet waters.

He restores my soul.

He guides me in paths of righteousness for His name's sake.

Even though I walk through the valley of the shadow of death,

I will fear no evil for you are with me.

Your rod and your staff, they comfort me."

That was David's song. This is mine.

———

My kids love fast food.

They are particularly fond of our local Whataburger. They love Whataburger.

When the boys were young, we made it our family ritual to buy whataburgers at the drive-thru on the way home from Sunday services. Sundays are busy days for us and this way, no one had to cook or clean following a meal.

But our ritual didn't stop there. As soon as we got home the guys, led by their dad, would strip out of their Sunday clothes and eat burgers and fries in front of the television, where we would watch the *NFL Game of the Week*.

It didn't get much better than that! That is, it didn't get much better than that for us guys. I can't say the same for my wife.

Guys love drive-thru burgers. They are practically a separate food group. But my wife is different. For some reason taking Carrie out to eat at Whataburger doesn't count as a date, even if we order in.

She prefers fine-dining. She wants conversation. She wants time alone, time away from the hustle and bustle of family life and work.

I am a follower of Christ Jesus. Like all true followers of Jesus, I have a relationship with the living God through Him.

Like all relationships, it has developed over time. As with all friendships, it matures through time, through time spent together.

Christians often call time alone with God their quiet time or devotional time or maybe even prayer time. The Bible says Jesus often withdrew to lonely places and prayed. It was His custom. It was His habit. This was no drive-thru experience. He was fine-dining with the Father in heaven.

People often speak with me about a decision they need to make or a circumstance they're walking through. I often ask them, "Have you prayed about it?"

Their answer of course is yes.

"I've been praying about this decision and I just don't know what to do," they say.

"How are you praying?" I ask.

"What do you mean?"

"How are you praying about this decision? How long have you been praying about this decision? How are you seeking God in this matter?"

I'm not trying to be difficult. I have just found that when we often say we're praying about something, we're not *really* praying. We're not withdrawing, talking and listening to what God might have to say. We're not reading the Bible, seeking a word from God.

We want to drive up, roll down the windows and tell Him what we want.

Shout our order into the speaker.

Pay at the next window.

Take the order to go.

We want a drive-thru Jesus.

———————

Fast food hasn't always been popular. When I was young, I could name only a few such places. People weren't as busy, weren't as rushed. There were more drive-ins than drive-thrus. And to be sure, we didn't eat out that much.

We ate at home..., around a table..., with the television off... and our shirts on. If the phone rang, we let it ring. They could always call back. Dinnertime was our time, our time together. We were dining in.

———————

Before I became pastor of Oak Ridge Church, I interviewed several times with a committee from the church. They were a great group of men, five in all. But one of them stood out to me immediately.

He was quiet. He didn't say much, but when he spoke he commanded the attention and respect of all who were in the room. He was very humble and wise. His name was Gene.

Gene would soon become one of my very best friends. He was at least fifteen years my elder. After I became pastor, Gene would call me nearly every Monday morning and ask, "How's my pastor doing today?"

I always looked forward to his call. He never had an agenda. He merely wanted to know how I was doing and how he could pray for me; how he could *really* pray for me.

Gene had a favorite verse of Scripture and everyone at the church knew what it was. It was a verse that described his demeanor, his lifestyle. You knew it was his favorite verse because he lived out that verse on a daily basis.

Gene's favorite verse was Psalm 46:10: "Be still, and know that I am God. I will be exalted among the nations. I will be exalted in the earth."

Be still.

Gene knew what it meant to be still. He knew what it meant to rest on the inside. He understood the difference between fast food and fine dining.

And what was his favorite verse has also become one of mine.

———

I don't think there is anything wrong with a little fast food. My credit - card receipts will back it up. And there is certainly nothing wrong with praying in the car on the way to work, or talking to God in the shower. I've learned to talk to God and look for God in almost everything I am doing. It's healthy. It's biblical.

But if you really want to know God more intimately, if you want a deeper relationship with Him, it's not going to happen at the drive-thru.

In a letter to the church at Laodicea, John was told to write these words of Jesus. "Here I am! I stand at the door and knock. If anyone hears my voice and opens the door, I will come in and eat with him, and he with me (Revelation 3:20)."

Laodicea was a church that had grown stale. Their temperature was lukewarm. Somewhere along the journey their love for Jesus had grown cold. Somewhere along the way they began driving through. And now Jesus was issuing the invitation to dine in: "I'm standing. I'm knocking. Will you answer the door"?

You have to be still. You need to look and listen. You will need to pull up a chair and see what God the Master Chef is preparing. He is taking everything – the good, the bad and the ugly – and blending it all together for good.

I realize upon reflection, this is what God has always been about. He has been using everything in my life to shape me more and more into His image. He is using His Word, different people, time in prayer and many of my experiences to prepare me for Him; to prepare me for His purposes. And He will continue to do so.

He is doing the same for you. That is who He is. That is what He does.

I am inviting you to pull up a chair and look over God's menu together with me. Let's see what God is serving up in our lives.

ORDERING

Presents.

My earliest memory is that of presents; not Christmas presents or birthday presents. My earliest memory is hospital presents.

I was three years old, lying in a hospital bed. As I raised my head and looked around the room, I remember seeing a large stack of presents. They were gifts people had brought to cheer me up I suppose.

I didn't know why all these people brought gifts, but they were stacked higher than my bed and for a kid, it doesn't get much better than that. *Why the gifts? Why this room? And why do I feel so dizzy? I think I will just lie back down.*

I had been in a wreck; a bad wreck.

Dad drove a Chevrolet pickup complete with a camper. He had just made his last payment. In the back of the truck were five gallon buckets of yellow paint he had just purchased for painting the church bus.

We finished eating at Burger King and were at a traffic light of a very busy intersection in Corpus Christi, Texas.

The light changed to green. We were the second car through the interchange. That's when it happened.

An ambulance carrying someone to a local hospital ran through a red light and smashed our truck from the side. There were four of us in the vehicle.

Mom's head hit the window. I fell to the floor. My sister fell on top of me. Dad kicked open the passenger side door so Mom could get out. The truck had spun around and through large concrete pillars where an overpass was being constructed. We painted the town yellow.

A passer-by took my father and me to a nearby hospital. A mailman who witnessed the accident took my mother and sister. I had lost consciousness and quit breathing. My father resuscitated me along the way.

For my parents it was a defining moment.

Mom was a homemaker. Dad worked multiple jobs. Later he would confide in her that he had seen everyone he loved almost taken away and he didn't even know them.

This accident was no accident. It served a great purpose in our family. It marked a re-ordering of priorities, a changing of the guard.

Experiences do this, you know. They cause us to examine what really is important in life.

Hospitals call it triage, deciding which patients to treat first based on the severity of the injury or illness.

Businesses often have stated goals based on their objectives and hopefully grounded in a mission or vision statement.

In baseball your order is the line-up. Who is hitting lead-off? Who is batting clean-up? Who will be my DH?

In our personal lives, order might be called priority and priorities are based on values. Order is essential. Values are paramount.

When asked which of the Jewish commandments was most important, Jesus said it was to love the Lord your God with all your heart, soul and mind. The second greatest was to love your neighbor as yourself. In terms of order: God first, others second. How we spend our time indicates if it is true.

———

While in seminary I attended a church with a large single adult group. I met a girl there that I really enjoyed. Her father was a pastor in the Midwest. I remember how surprised I was when she told me.

She was fun. She enjoyed life. She loved the Lord. She wasn't uptight and didn't have any real anger issues that I could see.

That caught my attention.

Here was a girl that grew up in a pastor's home, a pastor's daughter, and she enjoyed it. I had met a lot of pastor's kids before and most of them didn't like it. Seeing that I was studying for ministry and would likely one day be a pastor, husband and father, I had a few questions for her.

"What was the difference? Why did you enjoy growing up a pastor's daughter?"

I will always remember what she said to me.

"Two things," she said. "First, Dad was always the same at home as he was at church, as he was when he preached. And secondly, he always spent time with us. We always went on vacations together."

I think I learned more in that one conversation than in two semesters of Greek class.

———————

Later I would meet my wife Carrie. On our first date, I distinctly remember her ability to order – to order from a menu. She wasted no time. She opened the menu and quickly made her choice. She has always had the ability to make quick decisions. So much so, that I managed to somehow marry a woman who doesn't like to shop!

———————

Keith is one of my best friends. Several years back he lost his wife Linda, after 36 years of marriage, to an awful lung disease known as Idiopathic Pulmonary Fibrosis. She is one of the bravest and strongest individuals I have ever known. I witnessed the two of them travel an incredible journey as together they fought this debilitating illness for years.

Keith and I would talk, text and email almost daily. He always closed his emails with this signature: *Time flies. Spend it with those you love most.*

It does you know. Time flies. That's pretty much what the psalmist said when he wrote, "Teach us to number our days aright, that we may gain a heart of wisdom (Psalm 90:12)."

Unless your name is Methuselah and you live to be 969, you probably see life travelling at a faster pace than ever expected. That is, your life on earth.

And that's what we're talking about – your life, your time here on earth. It's an incredible gift and how we choose to spend the gift of time, how we choose to order our lives, says much about us.

My father learned that lesson early in my life and I was a beneficiary. We spent many hours together throwing, catching, working, fishing and hunting. Others have taught me that same truth through conversation and example.

Now I have opportunity to give the same gift to my wife, my children, and others I love. So do you. You have the opportunity to live life in the correct order; to love the Lord with all you have and to love others as yourself.

CHEROKEES, COLTS AND CHICKENS

Growing up, I loved playing baseball.

I played most sports at one time or another, but at the end of the day, my love was always baseball. Dad and I played a lot of catch in the back yard (remember the gift of time?). Every spring I played in the local *Little League*.

We had strange names for our teams back then. My first two years of prep ball I played on the Cherokees. Every team was an Indian tribe. We would chatter before every pitch like a tribal war party, "Hey batter, batter, batter, batter, batter; Hey batter, batter, batter, batter batter........SWING!"

We would chant that, along with a few other things, on every pitch. I don't know why, but that's what you did. We were the mighty Cherokees.

The following year I played on the minor league Colts. Our team was loaded. We won first place. We never lost once. At the end of every game our coach would give one game ball for outstanding play. He would write the score of the game on the baseball and write something about how well you did. Then he would sign the ball. I got the game ball twice. I still have them somewhere in my room back home.

Two of my favorite years were spent playing for the major league Bantams. In case you didn't know, and I'm guessing many people may not, a bantam is a chicken. In fact, it's a small breed of chicken.

Now who came up with that name I will never know. Why they came up with that name, I don't want to know. Maybe the board didn't like our manager or maybe we didn't sell enough raffle tickets. For whatever reason, we were the Bantams.

Looking back, the name didn't bother us at all. We thought Bantams were fighting chickens and people probably do fight those chickens in some countries. Or maybe that's just what our parents told us so we wouldn't think of ourselves as little chickens.

The first year on the Bantams was difficult. We won only a few games and were clearly not the class of the league. But year two was a different story. That was the year we strutted our stuff.

There were several good teams. Yet, we managed to stay undefeated in the first half of the season. The second half, though, belonged to the Aces. I think their coach must have been President of the Little League board or something. They were the Aces and we were the Fighting Chickens.

The mighty Aces defeated us soundly the second time around and we were dealt a winner-take-all championship game rematch. I spent all week thinking about that game.

School bragging rights were at stake, not to mention a coveted six-inch trophy. To say it plainly, it was a big deal.

Adding to the drama, we lost our best player and head coach. Our starting pitcher got in trouble at home and his parents decided to place him on the physically-unable-to-perform (PUP) list as punishment. Then, with about three weeks left in the season, our coach's job sent him out of town. What would happen next?

First, my Dad took over the reigns as team manager. As a shift worker in the local refinery, he somehow managed to give us the gift of time once more. And secondly, our infielder Tommy discovered a curveball.

But something else happened the week of the game.

It was Sunday morning. We were in church where a young man spoke as the guest. I don't remember his name or even why he was there. He was an athlete. He ran track at some university. And I will never forget his story.

Apparently he was a really good runner. He had his sights set on winning the gold medal in his event. But in his next-to-last meet he ran poorly. He felt he should have won his event, but that didn't happen. With one track meet remaining, he trained even harder.

He won his event at the next meet and came away with gold. And with great humility he began talking about the things God taught him through losing. He said that he could never have so greatly appreciated coming in first, without losing the week before.

After church I talked to my mom about what the man said. "Do you think that's something God might be teaching me? Do you think that might be the reason God allowed us to lose, so we might more greatly appreciate winning the championship tomorrow night?"

You have to admit, the timing of his message could not have been better. I thought that man's story was just for me. Besides, none of the boys who played on the Aces went to our church. So I'm not sure how God could have been saying that to them.

Of course my mom couldn't give me a straight-up yes to my question. No one, except the Lord, knew the answer. She heard the man speak and I'm certain she was thinking what I was thinking. But her best response was, "I don't know for sure. We just have to trust the Lord whatever happens."

The next day was game day. We decorated my dad's new Chevrolet pickup with signs and streamers. Dad always drove a Chevy. It was standing room only at the ballpark. I had never seen that many people at a Little League game.

And guess what?

The Mighty Chickens won! Tommy threw his newfound curveball. Our catcher hit a home run. The defense played flawlessly. We routed the Aces that night 9-0. From my shortstop position, it was beautiful.

All the guys jumped in the back of Dad's truck and rode to the local Dairy Queen where we ate banana splits and celebrated like champions.

Three different times in my Little League career I was part of a championship team. But this was by far my favorite. We pulled together, refusing to let defeat keep us down. And while no true competitor enjoys losing, we needed to lose that one game. I needed to lose that one game. I've always learned more when I lost. That's what the guy in church was saying the day before.

I don't like to lose. No one with any competitive nature enters a contest looking to lose. But God does teach us through defeat. We learn through losing. So I compiled my short list called Lessons in Losing.

- Losing improves my game. It drives me to become better. I can either settle for mediocrity or work to excel. Handled rightly, I become determined to improve.
- Losing reveals what is truly important in life. Unfortunately for many, it isn't until we lose something or someone that we realize their value. I once stood at the bedside of a man dying in the hospital, visiting with his estranged son. Years earlier they had a disagreement and hadn't spoken since. Now for the first time, he was meeting his grandchildren.
- Losing teaches me to trust God. There are many things we lean upon in life, but when all the supports are removed, all we have left is God. Then we learn to lean solely upon Him.
- Losing helps me deal with life in general. It isn't whether or not you will experience loss, but how you deal with loss as it occurs.

Nolan Ryan is one of the all-time great pitchers in Major League Baseball. I idolized him as a child and watched him pitch on several occasions. Nolan Ryan pitched in the majors for 27 years, struck out 5,714 batters and won 324 games. He also lost 292 times[1].

If you want to pitch in the big leagues, you had better learn to handle loss. If you want to learn and grow through life, you will need to learn through loss as well.

God continues to teach me through loss. I hope to teach my children through loss. It can be painful to watch our children lose at something, but if we always protect them from loss or prevent them from losing, we are setting them up for greater failure in the future. Losing is a reality of life.

In fact, we cannot experience a true life apart from losing. As Jesus one day said to His disciples, so he speaks to us today: "For whoever wants to save his life will lose it, but whoever loses his life for me will find it (Matthew 16:25)."

THANKSGIVING DAYS

Holidays have always been important.

Some of my fondest childhood memories occurred at Christmas, Easter, and Thanksgiving. Family was, and still is, important. Holidays were always times we gathered in large groups with aunts and uncles, grandmas and grandpas and nearby cousins.

That's what made this Thanksgiving different.

For some unknown reason, it was announced to us kids we would be spending Thanksgiving this year with Nanny. And to say it bluntly, I was disappointed.

Thanksgiving was almost always at our house. We ate, played football, ate some more and then watched football. We played ping-pong in the garage. We would draw names to exchange gifts come Christmas Eve.

And we're going *where* for Thanksgiving this year?

Nanny was my great-grandmother on my mother's side. She lived by herself in a small wood-frame house in Bishop, Texas. Her husband had died years earlier. He had worked in the local cotton gin.

I'm pretty sure we all got the "she-may-not-be-with-us-much-longer" speech, but as a nine year old boy, I really didn't think in those terms. I wanted to stay home, eat turkey, and play ping-pong.

It was November 28, 1974. A fresh cold-front had blown through our area and temperatures dropped that morning. We bundled up then loaded up the family car.

It was a twenty minute drive to Nanny's house. As we pulled up her home, you could see the excitement on her face. The table was beautifully decorated with china and better yet, it was loaded with food.

As I entered the house, there was a distinct odor I didn't recognize, but to this day will never forget – mothballs. They were everywhere! And the smell penetrated every corner of her home.

The house was laid with hardwood floors, the kind of floors everyone wants in their house today. Small area rugs and even smaller gas heaters could be found in nearly every room. It was cold.

After stuffing ourselves with a turkey dinner, we did what most Texans did at that time. We watched football. More specifically, we watched the Dallas Cowboys. They always played on Thanksgiving Day.

I was a huge fan of the silver and blue. I had my own helmet and home-made jersey. I would throw passes in the backyard pretending to be famed Cowboy quarterback Roger Staubach.

Nanny had one small television set that rested on a cart at the end of her bed. So we sat on the mattress, held to the covers and watched the most incredible Thanksgiving Day game.

The Cowboys were up against the rival Washington Redskins. Behind 16-3 in the third quarter, the immortal number 12, Roger the Dodger was knocked out of the game. As he was helped to the sidelines, all hope seemed lost. *Anyone up for a game of ping-pong?*

A rookie by the name of Clint Longley entered the game. And unbelievably, Longley quickly had the Boys back in the game. With 35 seconds remaining in the contest, he threw a game-winning 50-yard touchdown pass.

We jumped up and down and yelled in victory. We won! We won!

Clint Longley never played much after that. In fact, he played only one more season for the Cowboys, who then traded him to another team. Within two years of the Thanksgiving Day miracle, he was gone.

And so was Nanny. She died November 20, 1976.

———

Jeremiah 29:11 is one of the most beloved verses of Scripture. The verse offers hope. It speaks about a future. It tells how God has a plan and that His plan is good. It's a verse people want to know, people want to claim. It plainly states, "'For I know the plans I have for you,' declares the Lord. 'Plans to prosper you and not to harm you; plans to give you hope and a future.'"

Carrie and I had this verse printed on our wedding program. Isn't it funny how things rarely go according to *our* plans?

I first met Carrie at a wedding. She was a bridesmaid. I was the wedding singer. Her mother played the piano.

One year and a month later, we were married in the same church.

We invited a lot of people. Present wedding theory said about one-half of everyone you invite never attends the wedding. Apparently they didn't read the memo.

The church held about 350 people. 500 persons later our ushers were taking chairs from the preschool department.

A friend of ours offered to video the wedding as his gift to us. As my bride moved down the aisle a woman bumped the camera's tri-pod. We have a lovely picture of the church wall complete with audio.

With the wedding delayed 20 minutes, glass globes containing candles got overheated and began to break. Another candle wick burned too low and caught our greenery on-fire. And though few people at the time owned cell phones, we had one ring in the middle of our vows. It was a friend calling his wife to see how the ceremony had gone (apparently he did read the memo).

"For I know the plans I have for you," declares the Lord.

———————

Each year on our wedding anniversary, we disappear for a few days to celebrate our life together. One of our favorite cities to visit is San Antonio. There is a beautiful River Walk that runs through the heart of downtown. Restaurants, shops, hotels, and malls line its winding path.

Each year the city hosts one of the more unusual parades on Thanksgiving weekend. The parade floats literally float. Small barges, decorated by local businesses or organizations, motor single file down the river. Thousands of people crowd the downtown area to watch the parade. Good seats are at a premium.

One year my family was invited to the parade. As guests of a downtown business manager, we viewed the parade from a high veranda jutting out over the river. The view was spectacular. From our vantage point, we could see the boats coming well in advance. Unlike the crowds on ground level forced to watch the show one boat at a time, we could see much of the parade from beginning to end, sort of like God.

God is above time. He is what theologians call omnipresent. He is what we might call a time traveler. He sees the beginning as well as the end. That's what "eternal" means – without beginning, without end. He is the eternal God.

And we're not.

We don't see the end before it occurs. Like the crowds lined along the walk, we are forced to take life one step, one moment at a time. We walk by faith.

I may think I know what is best, but I don't, not really. My sight is so limited, but not God's. His view is perfect. And you can trust the One who knows all and sees all. He loves you and is working all things together for good – a Thanksgiving lesson I learned twice, thirty years apart.

Left to me, I wouldn't have traveled to Bishop. Left to me, I would have stayed home. Left to me, I would have missed my most memorable Thanksgiving Day.

Good thing it wasn't left to me.

"Trust in the Lord with all your heart and lean not on your own understanding: in all your ways acknowledge him, and he will direct your paths (Proverbs 3:5, 6 KJV)."

KEEPING IT BETWEEN THE LINES

I grew up on the water.

My parents built a modest home along the Nueces River, just miles upstream of the Nueces Bay. I loved to fish and swim in the river. I learned to water ski there also. Many times I camped along the water's edge in a tent with friends and fished through the night.

At age 16 I had my first real job. It, too, was on the water. It wasn't some run-of-the-mill job. This was a really sweet gig. I worked on a tugboat for my Uncle Bill.

The fact that I worked for my Uncle Bill tells you that I didn't get the job because of my expert seamanship or impressive resume. I got the job because he was my uncle.

Uncle Bill had been giving his nieces and nephews summer jobs for many years. Now it was my turn.

He owned a marine service, which among other things, towed barges throughout the port of Corpus Christi and the entire Texas coast. He captained the tugboat and for one summer, I was his primary deckhand. How cool is that?

I threw lines as we pulled up to loading docks and unhooked lines as we went underway. I cooked, cleaned, painted and did pretty much everything my Uncle Bill told me to do and everything my Uncle Bill didn't want to do.

I worked lots of hours and for a teenager, I made lots of money. I made twice what my friends were making and worked so much I didn't have time to spend my money.

My uncle constantly placed me in situations way over my head, far above my pay grade. He would simply walk away leaving me to figure things out.

I really enjoyed my job.

———

One night we were pushing a barge filled with fuel to an area just below Houston, Texas. It was a run we made several times that summer. All of our trips were made in the Texas Intracoastal Waterway, a 100 foot wide channel running the entire length of the Texas Coast.

I loved going to the front of the barge at night, away from most noises, where things were quiet and the night was pitch black. All you could see were stars or clouds or an occasional light somewhere off in the distance.

In the early hours of the night, as I was sleeping, I heard the captain blow the horn. It was my signal to come to the bridge.

Our spotlight had gone out. Aside from small running lights, it was the only real light on the boat. I climbed atop the upper deck to replace the bulb he assumed was bad. I discovered it wasn't the bulb, but faulty wiring.

"Come take the wheel," I was told. "I'll rewire the spotlight. You just watch this radar and keep it between the lines."

It was like playing a video game, just not a cool, modern video game with high definition graphics. It was more like *Pong*. There was a small circular screen with one line on the right and one line to the left with a small dot in the middle. The lines were the shore and our boat was the dot in the middle. *Just keep it between the lines.*

No problem. All was well. Who needed a light with this state-of-the-art, now totally obsolete radar system? *Just keep it between the lines.*

I was feeling pretty confident until I noticed something had changed. There was another dot. Something was invading my video game. To make matters worse, the new dot was bigger than my dot and headed straight toward my dot!

I was about to tell the captain about this big dot, when a blinding flash lit up the sky. It was the spotlight of another tug pushing a larger barge. Words were not needed, though a few were exchanged.

We were headed north while he was travelling south. And while 100 feet may be room enough for an experienced tugboat captain, it seemed like inches from my captain's chair.

Stay calm. Trust your instruments. Just keep it between the lines.

I safely steered past, while the captain rewired the spotlight. Most importantly, we avoided the front page of the *Houston Chronicle*.

———————

Jesus was a carpenter by trade. Yet, He spent much time on the water. Disciples like Peter, James, Andrew, and John were all fishermen. And since Jesus was all about spending time with them, He was often found on the lake. And like my Uncle Bill, He often put His disciples in situations way over their heads.

Like the time Jesus fed thousands of people with one boy's lunch. The crowd was overwhelmed by his power to multiply fish and chips.

Immediately, the Bible says, Jesus *made* His disciples get back in the boat and row to the other side. He then dismissed the crowd and went up a mountainside to pray.

The disciples were caught in a storm, unable to row against wind and waves. They were in a storm because Jesus sent them into the storm. And from His summit view, Jesus witnessed the entire event, praying for them each by name: "Help them Father, to keep it between the lines."

Eventually Jesus reached out to them, walking atop the water. As He climbed into their skiff, the winds weakened and waves ceased. His disciples worshipped Him saying, "Truly, you are the Son of God (Matthew 14:33)."

———————

Many times I have heard people say that Jesus will never give us more than we can handle. I know what they are trying to say. It's a statement made often in the midst of a storm or crisis, telling ourselves (or someone else) that everything is going to be okay.

But I believe that God does, many times, give us more than *we* can handle; the key word being *we* – you and me. He places us in situations that we, in our own strength, cannot handle. He sends us into storms *we* cannot row against.

He wants us to trust Him completely. He wants us to rest in Him.

While the storm is too great for us, nothing is too difficult for God. He will never give us more than *He* can handle. That is the truth He wants us to know and experience. We can do all things through Christ who gives us strength.

Yield to Him.

———

I still enjoy being around the water.

I love to swim and love to fish. I love taking the kids to the pool, watching them as they enjoy the water, too.

But I can't stand the kiddy pool.

The kiddy pool is nasty. The kiddy pool is dirty and warm. The kiddy pool is filled with chlorine to keep bacteria in check. Besides all this, God doesn't *want* you in the kiddy pool.

You were made for the deep. You were designed for the high dive. God wants you in over your head, so you might learn to swim. It is only in the deep that we witness the power of God working through us. Only in the depths do we truly experience God.

I am pretty sure the reason we believe God will never give us more than we can handle, is because mostly we attempt things we can handle. We tell others we are trusting God while carrying a back-up plan in our hip pocket in case He doesn't come through. Of that I am often guilty.

———————

I enjoyed my days on the tugboat. I learned many life-lessons on the bays. Today, I drive over the same port regularly as I travel throughout the area. Many times I look down from the bridge and see the same boats on which I used to work.

A tugboat is smaller than the larger ships coming to port, a mere fraction of their size. But they have an important role. The larger ships are carrying cargo from long distances. They maneuver well upon the open sea. But narrow inlets are a different story. Large, ocean-going vessels can't steer in tight places. They need help. They need a guide. And so the tugs come alongside and safely deliver them to the docks.

I have found that I don't navigate well in tight places either. Not unlike the ships in port, I need a guide. I need a helper. And God the Father has just the Person. He is the Holy Spirit.

The Holy Spirit is my Guide, my Helper, and my Counsel. The Greek word is paraclete which literally means "one who comes alongside another". He comes alongside to help you, to guide you, to comfort, and give you counsel.

He enables you to keep it between the lines.

Yield to His leadership. Let Him throw His lines upon you. Learn from Him, for He is gentle and humble and you will find rest in Him.

LETTERS OF REMEMBRANCE

I remember the very first letter I ever received. I had no idea what it said. I was too young to read, but I still recognized my name on the envelope.

Mail was a big deal when I was young. People wrote letters to each other – actual hand-written letters filled with meaningful stuff. Today it's just credit card apps and bills. If you want to communicate with someone you just call or text from your cell phone, or maybe send an email. I think my kids are really missing out on something by not writing and receiving letters. Many are technologically savvy but relationally starving.

I was the first one to the mailbox that day and amidst the letters was one addressed to me. It was from a relative asking me to be in a wedding. They wanted me to be the ring bearer.

Now I had no idea why they wanted a bear at their wedding or why they would want me to dress like a bear. I didn't even own a bear costume. But I thought the idea of dressing up like a bear and showing up at their wedding sounded pretty cool.

I was more than disappointed once I learned I had to wear a Sunday suit instead of a bear suit. But reluctantly I agreed (like I had any say in the matter).

The wedding was terrible.

It was in a tiny rock church with a metal roof. To make matters worse, it started raining. Then it began hailing. It was so loud you could barely hear. This huge storm was rocking the little church. I started crying and went to sit in the front row with the mother-of-the-groom.

My first experience on stage was a disaster.

———

When I went off to college, I still looked for letters. I lived in a large college dormitory on the campus of the University of Texas. The mailroom was a popular place. We checked our mail daily looking for letters from friends or family.

My roommate was my best friend in high school. We had gone to church together since we were kids. We played baseball and suffered through football. And now we were studying engineering together at the same school.

Anytime one of us received a letter, we would read it aloud and think about those back home. We had a telephone in the room, but I don't remember using it all that much like someone might today. I think that's one reason letters were so special.

I remember one letter from Grandma. She wrote to tell me how proud she was of me and enclosed a ten dollar bill.

"Sending you just a little gift," she said. "Maybe take your little girlfriend out for a Blizzard?"

Way to go Grandma. I still have the letter.

I have letters from my college days and letters I received while in seminary. I have a bunch of letters and cards from my wife while we were dating. I'm not going to tell what's written inside those, but I still have them.

———

As a pastor, I occasionally attend conferences. When I go to a conference, I generally try to find one or two things that make the trip worthwhile. Speakers usually give so much advice it can be overwhelming. I look to implement only a few ideas, something learned at the expense of another.

Of all things the speaker said at one such conference, I took away one nugget of truth. He called it his encouragement file. The Encouragement File is a collection of letters, cards or notes, anything written to encourage you.

I have been keeping one ever since. It's the fattest file folder in the cabinet.

I have cards from people thanking me for helping them through hard times. Some are letters of appreciation. I have the local newspaper clipping announcing my first day as pastor of our church. Today, I barely recognize the guy in the photo.

There are pictures that kids have colored for me in Sunday School and even a few birthday cards. I have this torn piece of notepad from a then 90-year-old man. He had one of the best gardens in town. Scratched out in pen are the words: "Preacher, come by and see what we can get out the ice box" – Ernie.

I had the honor of leading his funeral service 8 years later.

———————

A number of books in the New Testament are letters. They are real letters to real people in real places. Paul wrote letters, John wrote letters, and so did Peter. Letters were rare in those days, usually delivered by a trusted friend. When I study the New Testament letters, I imagine people gathered in a room listening as someone reads the letter aloud. Paul often asked that the same letter be read to other churches.

And while Paul wrote for various reasons, one of his greatest purposes for writing was to encourage. "Keep going. Stand firm. Be strong. Keep gathering. I'm praying for you."

You can *think* good things about people, but unless your thoughts are spoken, written or in some way communicated directly to them, your thoughts are useless. You need to tell them. You need to encourage them.

When you encourage someone, you are "instilling courage". You are giving them courage to continue moving forward. Life takes courage.

The single mom needs courage to parent. The man diagnosed with cancer needs courage for treatment. The Christian student needs courage to walk the halls of the local high school.

I thank the Lord for all my encouragers, for all who took time to send a letter, write a card, dial my number or offer a positive word. They have taught me an important lesson about the power and value of words. Don't just think good things about others. You need to tell them, because life can be a bear.

BIG MIKE

I am amazed at the people who have crossed my path at critical intersections in life. As I entered junior high, I met Big Mike.

I have always loved working with junior high kids. It's an awkward time in life. You're not a teenager but, you're not a child either. You're a tweener, stuck 'tween stages in life.

To make matters worse, I was a little tweener. I was what people affectionately refer to as a late-bloomer. I played basketball in junior high. My coach listed me at 5'4". I never broke 5 foot until high school, something my kids still laugh about today.

But one Sunday this little tweener went to church and met Big Mike. He was our new Youth Minister. He liked sports. He played college football. He sang and played the guitar, too. He was a pied piper. Kids gravitated toward Mike and I was no different.

I would later work with teenagers in a similar capacity. I think Mike had something to do with that.

Our church never had a Youth Minister on staff that I could remember. Mike came at the beginning of my 7th grade year and would leave six years later as I went off to college. Once more, he was someone willing to give me the gift of his time.

He would come and visit us at our school. No one from church ever came to the school cafeteria. But Mike did and it wasn't for the food. He would sit down and visit with students and visit with my friends. That made me uncomfortable at first. I was used to talking with Mike at church, not school.

I wasn't a bad kid that lived one way at school and one way at church. I chose my friends pretty wisely. I knew who to run with and who to run from. But when Mike started showing up at school it sort of bridged a gap that I had left opened.

One morning at church our Sunday School teacher was out. He was probably sick or on vacation or maybe he had to work. Mike taught our class in his absence that day.

It was a boy's class – filled with boys I had known much of my life. We sat in the room looking at each other in our familiar circle of chairs. That's when Mike told us to get our Bibles and go the church van. He took us to breakfast that morning.

We sat at a table and drank orange juice while Mike taught the lesson. It was strange. I remember looking around to see who else might be there. Once more he made me uncomfortable. I wasn't ashamed of my faith, or at least I didn't think I was. But I kept wondering what others were thinking about these Christians studying the Bible at a restaurant?

Mike was closing the gap.

He was good at that. He didn't separate the sacred from the secular or the church house from the school house. His approach to youth ministry exposed something in me I didn't want to see. I compartmentalized my faith.

Like a neatly packed refrigerator/freezer, I had a place for everything. School went in this compartment and home-life had its own container. Faith was on the top shelf, but not to be mixed with the others. I struggled to keep things stocked together.

But Mike didn't.

And more importantly, neither did Jesus. He was a bridge builder, too.

Jesus taught large groups of people. He fed thousands at a time. Sometimes entire villages or towns would bring their sick to Jesus. He would stay up all night healing them. But while Jesus would minister to the crowds, His main focus was always the small group, including an inner circle of twelve men he was training.

Jesus didn't often teach in a classroom or synagogue. He taught in the grain fields or in a boat or on a hillside. With Jesus, it was OJT ATT. He was out and about where people lived, where people worked. He went to weddings, feasts and religious celebrations.

Jesus was always bridging the gap.

———

I currently live in a small community of 20,000 called Portland. It's a great place to live on the Gulf Coast. When I tell people I live in Portland their first question is, "Portland, Oregon? Portland, Maine?"

I live in Portland, Texas.

Portland, Texas is a bedroom community for the largest city in our area, Corpus Christi (which means the body of Christ). And to the people of Corpus Christi, I live across the bridge.

You see, to get to Portland you have to cross the bridge, the Harbor Bridge. It is nearly 250 feet tall and 600 feet long, spanning the Port of Corpus Christi. And while I love living in Portland, I have met many people who will not live here. They are afraid to daily cross the bridge.

I used to feel that way, too.

Extravagant acts gain your attention. When someone does something so out of the ordinary, you take notice. Days before the crucifixion of Jesus, a woman named Mary did something very costly.

Jesus was a guest in the home of Mary, Martha and their brother Lazarus. Jesus was reclining at the table while the meal was being served. That's when it happened.

"Mary took about a pint of pure nard, an expensive perfume; she poured it on Jesus' feet and wiped his feet with her hair. And the house was filled with the fragrance of the perfume (John 12:3)."

The perfume was expensive, worth nearly an annual salary. As nard, it carried a strong, pungent odor, lasting for days. Martha wiped the feet of Jesus with her hair. And the house never smelled the same. Neither did His feet.

A few days later, Jesus was unjustly whipped, beaten and cruelly crucified. As he hung on the cross, I believe the odor remained. The aroma of her actions on Monday permeated the cross on Friday.

———————

The Bible declares that "you are a chosen people, a royal priesthood, a holy nation, a people belonging to God, that you may declare the praises of him who called you out of darkness into his wonderful light (1 Peter 2:9)." Followers of Jesus are called priests and together we form a royal priesthood.

In Latin, the word priest literally means "bridge builder".

Jesus is declared in Scripture as The Great High Priest, the ultimate Bridge Builder, spanning the gap between man and God. Jesus is God in human flesh and has invited us all to come to the Father through Him, through the cross. He wants all to cross-over.

Before ascending to heaven, He entrusted His followers with the task of building bridges to others. They were given the responsibility of sharing His blueprint for living.

His plans are too great to keep to ourselves. They are meant to be shared, to be told, by bridge builders like you, like me, like Big Mike.

This is what people want to see. This is what people *must* see – a faith in Jesus that is celebrated on Sunday, and fleshed out on Monday and Tuesday and Wednesday and Friday; a faith that will permeate every aspect of our lives.

It's travelling with Jesus wherever we go, whenever we go; and refusing to live in fear of bridges that exist.

Cross over.

PHYSICS 301

I'm not good at taking risks.

I know that sounds terrible, but it's true. It's not easy for me to take a risk and that just shouldn't be. I admire people who take risks. And considering the fact that the most enjoyable times of my life have come when I have taken the greatest risk, this should encourage me to take even more risks.

Why don't I take more risks?

It wasn't always this way for me though. I used to be bold. I used to throw caution to the wind and set sail. Sometimes I see that same entrepreneurial spirit rise up within me, but not nearly enough.

Like the day I left for college.

Ever since I was a young boy, ever since I could remember, I wanted to attend the University of Texas. I really don't know how to explain it, but I knew early on where I was going to school. There was little doubt.

Neither of my parents attended college. No one in my immediate family ever went to the University of

Texas. But that's where I was going. For me, it felt almost pre-determined.

My college roommate was my best friend in high school. My youngest sister transferred to UT that same semester. All three of us caravanned to Austin on the same afternoon. With the empathy of an 18 year old kid, I remember looking back wondering why my mother was crying as we left the driveway.

I was excited. I was on an adventure. I was going to Texas! *This is why I studied hard in high school, right? Remember telling me you never went to college and all your kids were going to college? Well, I'm going to college.*

My first two years in college I lived on-campus. It was a coed dorm with thousands of residents, so large we had our own zip code. I lived on an all-men's floor with a community bath. I bought the full meal deal at the school cafeteria. Life was great. I didn't have to clean my bathroom or cook any meals. If I wanted clean sheets I simply took them to the laundry room and got new ones, which I did at least twice a semester whether I needed to or not. All I had to do was my laundry and my homework.

I worked hard every summer, saved all my money and then gave it all to the university for my room, board, and education. I received quite an education.

I was an engineering major in college. I was good at math, enjoyed numbers and figured God had given me this ability for some reason. So I studied engineering.

One of my first classes was Physics 301. I say class, but in reality it was a lecture hall built much like a movie theater with rows of seats climbing at a steep angle.

I chose the front row.

With over 300 people in the class I wanted the professor to know my face and name. Besides, I'm a little too ADD to sit on any back row. I have to be up front. It's not enough for me to see and hear. I have to feel. I have to be involved. I am what people call a kinesthetic learner.

The bell rang. The professor welcomed us all to campus and to Physics 301. Then with the same empathy I had toward my mother he announced, "70% of you will fail this class. Less than one-third will survive. So you three on the front row (pointing to me) wave goodbye to the next seven people in your row. They won't be here by semester's end."

I laughed, but inside I was afraid he might be right. And he was.

The day after our first major exam, the class was half-empty. Following the second exam, half of that half was gone. Fortunately I was still sitting on the front row believing that was where I belonged.

I went to the professor's office following the first exam. You would think with all the students it would be nearly impossible to see him. But it wasn't. In fact, I never had trouble visiting with a professor in college. I guess people were either too afraid, didn't care or thought he was too busy to give the time of day. But I never found professors to be that way.

They were always approachable and I don't recall standing in too many lines. I visited my physics professor several times that semester and at the end of the semester he told me a story.

He would always announce before each exam that cheating would not be tolerated. He had teaching assistants watching the crowd and if caught, you would be removed from class if not the university. More than a dozen people were caught cheating on the first exam.

For the second exam, he used cameras. He announced that the exam was being recorded and would be reviewed by assistants. "Don't cheat because you will get caught."

Once more a handful of desperate people took their chances and lost. They were expelled from class. Yet, all these were trumped when on the night of the final, a man sent his wife, along with his ID, to take his exam. Who would have thought? Why take such a risk?

A.W. Tozer once wrote, "What comes into our minds when we think about God is the most important thing about us."[2] And for what it's worth, I think he was right.

So many people I meet feel that God is sort of like my professor standing over them, watching their every move, waiting for them to make a mistake, eager to say, "Aha! I caught you. Get out of my class."

To be sure, God does see everything. His knowledge is perfect and He is without limit. Nothing escapes His view. You really can't cheat on God. And one day, the Bible says, we will all stand before Him.

But He wants you to pass. He wants you to safely cross over. You can't earn that privilege nor do you deserve it.

God is not grading on a curve of merit. He offers eternal life by grace through faith in His Son.

And with faith there is risk. But it's a risk worth taking, a risk producing great reward. As a young boy I took that risk and placed my faith in Christ as Savior. In fact, I didn't think of it as risk at all. It all made perfect sense. It still makes perfect sense.

What doesn't make sense is my lack of risk-taking today.

When you take a risk, by definition you are exposing someone or something you value to danger or loss. Actually, you are exposing these to the *possibility* of danger or loss.

So I began asking myself, "What prevents risk? What prevents the born-again follower of Christ, who has risked all by trusting in Jesus, from taking risks on a daily basis?"

<u>Control.</u> The very idea of risk involves letting go, or loosening your grip. You may love your life as it is, or enjoy the wealth that you have obtained, and the last thing you want to do is turn that loose. Jesus warned us, "Whoever finds his life will lose it, and whoever loses his life for my sake will find it (Matthew 10:39)." Hand over the controls.

<u>Fear.</u> There is a fear of loss or a fear of failure. What if we risk and lose? What if we risk and make fools of ourselves? We don't know what the end result might be, and we fear what we don't know or understand. John writes, "There is no fear in love. But perfect love drives out fear (1 John 4:18)."

<u>Age.</u> For most people, the older you get, the less risk you take. Every financial advisor will tell you to take less risk with age. When you are young you don't mind risk because there always seems time to make up for any loss. As you grow older the time grows short.

A lack of faith. For the follower of Christ, it is all about faith, or a lack of faith. Scripture says, "So then, just as you received Christ Jesus as Lord continue to live in him (Colossians 2:6)." How did you receive Christ Jesus as Lord? You received Him by faith. How should you continue to live? Continue to live in faith.

Two basic questions lay at the heart of risk-taking. (1) "Is God calling me to this? Is this something God is asking me to risk?" And (2), "Do I trust God to provide?"

It is faith; plain, simple faith. And "the righteous will live by faith (Habakkuk 2:4)."

It's not rocket science. It's not even Physics 301.

TEXAS SUNSETS

Texas has long been known for beautiful sunsets. Along the coast, they can simply be spectacular. Being a flatlander and all, I can see the horizon for miles. It is not unusual to see a spectrum of colors jutting through tall clouds or open skies as evening approaches.

In my final semester of college, I came to the understanding that God was calling me to serve Him in Christian ministry. I didn't know how I would serve, only that I was to serve. I graduated with my Bachelors of Science in Mechanical Engineering and headed off to seminary.

I quickly found a few guys looking for a roommate. Rent was cheap and that was good. Next, I needed a job.

People love to hire seminary students. They are honest, hardworking individuals. I went to the school job board filled with requests for workers. I wrote down names and phone numbers and made a few calls.

There was a widow near the school who needed yard care. I went to her house the next day to begin working. I mowed her yard, trimmed trees and worked her flower beds. It was about a 5 to 6 hour job. She paid minimum wage. It wasn't much but I didn't need much. I had always been taught, it's always easier to find a job when you have a job.

It was a typical hot summer day in Texas. As I finished up her flower beds I sat down for a moment and watched the sun beginning to set.

There are moments in life we call defining moments. Some people call them spiritual markers. I don't exactly know how to explain it, but this was one of those intersections where many of my thoughts came together.

Up to this moment, my trek to seminary was an adventure. I had no idea what the next day might hold, or from where my next job might come. But it really didn't matter. I lived one day at a time and was content to do so.

But as I sat on this woman's porch with $30 in my pocket, I stared deeply into the horizon and for the first time thought, *"What on earth are you doing here?"*

I have a bachelor's degree from a major university and I just worked six hours for minimum wage. Are you kidding me? I have three years of schooling still ahead to graduate from seminary. What am I thinking?

I wanted to cry. Okay, I admit it, I cried. Not some sobbing, wailing cry for all the neighborhood to hear, but tears came to my eyes.

I was experiencing a major course correction in my life and now, for the first time, reality was setting in. It was my own personal pity party and fortunately, it didn't last too long.

People will often ask after learning I graduated an engineering major, "Wasn't it hard to turn your back on that? Wasn't it difficult to leave all that money on the table to study ministry?" And with all honesty my answer has always been no. But if you had asked me in that moment, I may have said yes.

Yes it can be difficult. Yes there are those moments. And yes, there have been similar moments, but none quite as strong. Like the time I quit going to classes for a few weeks to remind myself just why I was there. Or the time a woman scolded me for the way she felt her daughter was being treated in our youth ministry. There are times when people leave the church because of a decision that was made. These are the moments when I think to myself, "I didn't sign up for this."

But I did. And so did you, if you are a follower of Christ.

Every follower of Jesus accepts the same invitation: "Come, follow me."

Jesus invited Andrew, Peter, James and John. They left the fishing business and followed Jesus. Matthew left his tax collector's booth. He was so excited he threw a big party so his friends could meet Jesus as well. Each of His disciples surrendered everything in favor of the call – "Come, follow me." They each would die a martyr's death.

I'm many years removed from that seminary sunset. But occasionally the Lord takes me there again.

I once attended a two-day leadership conference filled with some pretty big names both in the church and in the marketplace. But one speaker, unknown to most of us, grabbed my attention more than any other.

She spoke of her service among the poor. She had left a prestigious university to work with those in her country who had nothing, who literally ate garbage. I was captivated by her humility even more than her words. Her life spoke volumes.

Following her speech, everyone attending the conference was given a piece of broken pottery and a pen. After an additional challenge, we were told to write something on the clay shard. I knew exactly what I was to write.

God didn't audibly tell me to write these words, but He may as well have. There was no doubt, no hesitation. And so I wrote, "Come. Follow Me".

I was visibly shaken for the next twenty minutes. There was a thirty minute intermission and people went to the foyer to visit. I couldn't leave. I could only pray and weep.

A few days later I received a phone call. It was a friend, once a member of our church who had moved to the east coast. After some catching up, he got straight to the point. The church he was attending was looking for a pastor. He and his wife, after praying together, felt led to call and ask me to forward a resume to them.

Could this be why God had me etch those words just days earlier? I admit I didn't want to pack and move my family 1500 miles to the eastern United States. But I felt I had no choice. "Come. Follow Me."

I forwarded a resume soon thereafter, thinking nothing else would happen, hoping nothing else would happen. And then one evening I received a phone call asking for more information. And once more, reluctantly, I sent it. For me, merely sending that information was a gut-wrenching decision.

I never heard any more from that church, though I have visited with my friend several times since then. The church called another man to be their pastor, and honestly I was glad. The entire experience, spread out like a blanket for several months, was both difficult and revealing.

What happened to the guy who took his bachelor's degree and vaulted for seminary? What happened to the risk-taker who lived one-day-at-a-time? I had turned from the man who doubled five talents to one who left his talent with the banker for mere interest. I should have gladly said, "Lord, Your will be done. More than anything else, I want to follow You."

I believe the Lord's will was ultimately accomplished. I also believe I failed a test.

It was easier to risk, to trust, when I was younger. As a single man I could live on beans and weenies and hoe gardens for a meager income. But as a husband and father of five, I have to trust God for them as well. My decisions, my actions, now carry greater impact.

Can we even fathom how Abraham felt when God told him to take his son, his only son Isaac, and sacrifice him on Mount Mariah? He had no idea there would be a ram caught in a nearby thicket. He didn't raise the knife thinking this was merely a test. The Bible says "Abraham reasoned that God could raise the dead (Hebrews 11:19)." No wonder he is called the father of all who believe.

The Bible tells us the disciples were called Christians first at Antioch (Acts 11:26). It wasn't a name they gave themselves. It was given them by others, and likely not as a compliment. People called them Christians because they followed the teachings of Christ. But before they were known as Christians, they were called Followers of the Way.

I like that name. I like the title "Followers of the Way". The term Christian is great, but it seems to have a different meaning to different people. "I live in America. Therefore, I am a Christian." Or, "I go to such and such church. I am a Christian." Some believe, "I'm a really good person. I am a Christian."

But at the heart of the word Christian is the fact that we are followers of Christ. We follow the person and teachings of Jesus Christ. And we have given our lives to follow Jesus, who is the Way, the Truth and the Life. We are followers of the Way.

Followers of the Way do not allow their lives to be defined by a title they hold, or a job they perform. They are not hanging their hats on family lineage or church attendance. It is clear to others who they are by the way they walk. Their footsteps leave an undeniable imprint: We are followers of Jesus.

When God flooded the earth, saving only Noah and his family, along with a bunch of birds and animals, He gave them a sign once the waters receded. The rainbow, which arched across the sky, was God's promise to Noah, and to us all, that He would never again flood the earth. Any time

Carrie and I are out with the kids and a rainbow appears we remind them of God's promise to all mankind.

But each time I witness a gorgeous sunset, the Lord gives me a more personal reminder: "Come. Follow Me."

And in His strength, I will.

PIZZA & BEER

Seminary was overall, a great experience. Some of the coolest guys I know I met during those years. Here was a group of people gathered from all over the United States, to study and prepare for a life of Christian ministry. Once we broke the huddle we were spread throughout the nation and world.

I keep in touch with very few of them. That's unfortunate I think. Yet, life goes on and I am certain we will have an eternity to talk about our adventures. There was a time during those years, however, in which I got tired of being around all these ministry students. I felt suffocated.

I like to build friendships with people and through those friendships, introduce them to the person of Jesus. But all my friends already knew of Jesus. They were Christians. They were Followers of the Way. I needed to find some friends who were not believers.

I began working at an adolescent psychiatric care center to support myself through school. I was working with at-risk teenagers, but the center itself wasn't faith-based.

There were some really nice people who worked there and cared about helping teens.

I had been praying about how to form friendships with people who may not be followers of Christ. Soon, one of the men I worked with asked me if I wanted to play softball. He was on a competitive co-ed softball team looking for another player.

I loved to play softball and was a good player. After all, I had been a member of the Mighty Chickens back in the day.

I showed up for the first game and quickly realized, *God has answered my prayer.* He put me on a fun-loving, beer-drinking, potty-mouthed team. Actually, they weren't that bad. I had so much fun playing with them.

It was a strange breath of fresh air. I was getting stifled by all those straight-laced, brief case-totin' Bible students back at school and hadn't even realized it. As far I knew there were only two Christians on this team!

One night after the game I was walking across the parking lot with one of the players. All the other team members were sitting on the back of their cars drinking beer out of the trunk. It was the usual post-game ritual.

"Hey," they called out to us. "We're going out for pizza and beer. You guys want to come?" Now neither of us had ever stayed after and drank with the team, so I thought it was pretty nice of them to ask. Still, I had things to do like study the New Testament and the life of Jesus for class the next day.

But before I could say anything, my friend said, "No thanks. I don't drink. I'm a Christian." Now there's a line you might want to keep to yourself. The look on their faces said it all.

Without hesitating they looked at me. "How about you Mark? Do you want to go?"

"You bet," I said. "Where are we going?"

I had to get some gas and make one stop. By the time I had caught up, the team had pulled several tables together and had their first drink. "Come sit on this end of the table," someone said. "All the smokers are at the other end."

I sat down, ordered a coke and jumped right into the conversation. It was great and things were about to get even better.

I was sitting next to one of the women who played on the team along with her boyfriend. "So you say you go to school here," she asked. "Where do you go?"

"Well," I said, "I attend the Baptist seminary."

"What's a seminary?" she questioned.

That was actually a great question. I didn't even know what a seminary was until someone told me I ought to attend one when I was called to ministry.

"It's where people study who are going into Christian ministry."

"Oh, so you're going to be a priest?"

"Not exactly. But I hope to serve in a church someday."

"I grew up Catholic," she said. "What do Baptists believe? You guys don't drink and dance and stuff like that, right?"

"You know," I explained. "It's not so much about being Baptist or Catholic. It's about what you believe of God; what you believe about Jesus."

She was actually listening. She sincerely wanted to know what I believed.

So I continued. "There's a great question I like to ask a person that sort of puts everything in perspective for us all. It's this: If you were to stand before God right now and He asked you, 'Why should I let you into heaven?' What would you say?"

Suddenly the table got really quiet, like when you are shouting to someone over the music and suddenly the music stops and you're still shouting. Everybody looks at you and wonders why you're talking so loud.

You could have heard a pin drop. Everyone talking stopped talking; everyone eating stopped eating. The Holy Spirit was quieting the crowd to hear the answer to everyone's $60,000 question.

I will never forget how this woman looked straight at me and with great honesty said, *"I don't know what I'd say. I have never thought about that."*

For the next 10 minutes I was able to explain God's plan for all of us. I was able to tell the team what I call "the story of the Bible in a nutshell." It was a divine appointment set around pizza and beer.

There at the table, people were hearing about God's purpose for all of us and the hope we can have now in Jesus. I don't remember what I scored the next day on my Bible exam, but the evening was a homerun.

———

In the New Testament, Jesus was often opposed by a group of religious leaders known as Pharisees. From what I can tell, many of them were sincere in their attempts to be right before God. We always fault them for their legalism and they were certainly legalistic when it came to keeping God's law.

But their legalism led them to something even worse – isolation. They isolated themselves from people. They distanced themselves from others who were not like them, who didn't hold similar beliefs, and ate pizza and drank beer. Their team cheer was, "We don't dance. We don't chew. We don't go with the girls who do." (It's something my dad used to say.)

The point is, if you have what others need, why keep it from them? How can you help someone if you're not willing to spend time with them? You might as well say, "No thanks. I can't hang with you. I'm a Christian."

Really?

In Scripture, Jesus is called "a friend of sinners (Matthew 11:19)." It wasn't a name given in kindness, but one tossed out like a fading jab. But I like that name, friend of sinners. I like the fact that Jesus spent time with those who needed him most; those whom the religious leaders called sinners.

He ate in their homes, sailed in their boats. He attended their parties and weddings, feasts and festivals. He went there, because they were there – people who needed him were there.

To be fair, Jesus spent most of His time with his disciples. He literally poured His life into a handful of men, but not to the neglect of others.

———

I have a confession. Someone has said it is good for the soul. I confess that I love my church. I love going to church. I love being with the church. Something seems very wrong if I'm not at church on Sunday morning. Everything makes sense to me, from the music to the message, from the offerings to the invitation. I get it.

But often I find myself on the front row of our church, in the middle of a chorus or hymn that we're singing and I wonder, *"Does this make sense to the guy who is here for the first time? The neighbor that our friends brought to church, the one who said she hasn't been to church since she was a child, what does she make of all this?"*

There are times I listen to someone preaching on television (I don't do that very much), and I say to myself, *"No wonder people don't go to church. This is terrible."*

A tension begins tugging from opposite ends. I see the church's need to connect with its surrounding community. If my neighbor, who has lived next door since 2010, visits my church that is still operating like it is 1970, he is asking himself, "What's wrong with these people? What are they doing?" And the connection is lost because methods have been placed on shelves higher than the message. Our opinions are held equal with truth.

But I feel a pull in another direction. The church is supposed to be different. We are not the same. We are set apart for the Lord and His purposes. We are called to be holy and that very term means "to be set apart". We should look different because there is something different about us. We are Followers of the Way. And too often the church, in her attempts to become so relevant to her culture, has lost her relevance and purpose.

So what's the church to do?

Follow Jesus and connect with others.

Jesus tells us to "go and make disciples of all nations (Matthew 28:19)." He emphasized going rather than bringing, engaging over inviting. He didn't mail out multi-colored postcards with cute little pictures inviting them to hear a relevant message. He ate at their tables and taught in their homes and spoke hope into their lives.

And while I'm not saying our uses of media and technology are wrong, I am saying that somewhere along the way, we may have allowed them to surpass the most basic, effective form of connecting with others – through relationships. Who am I building a friendship with right now, through which I can share the hope of Jesus?

I am always challenging our church to share Jesus with their friends. And many of them have the same problem I had back in seminary. They have few friends that are not already believers. Their closest friends are in their church or other churches. And on the one hand that is good. We tend to become like those we are with. "Bad company corrupts good character (1 Corinthians 15:33)."

But how will we ever connect with unbelievers apart from friendships? Without that connection our churches become book clubs where, with the best of intentions, we gather to study the Book with other members of the club.

I keep a journal. I am not as consistent as some I know, but I have been keeping a journal off and on for years. They are not fancy. Many of my journals are simple notebooks bought at the school supply aisle of the local store.

In the back of my journal I keep various lists. One of those lists contains friends of mine who never attend church or may not know Jesus as Savior. I pray for them. I stay in touch with them. I try to connect with them. I want to know what they might say if they were stand before God right now and He asked them why He should let them in heaven. I want them to know Jesus.

Who are *you* building a friendship with *right now* so you might share with them the hope of Jesus?

LITTLE BY LITTLE

The words jumped from the page.

Carrie and I had been married only a short while, living in a two bedroom apartment. I was on a church staff, working primarily with students.

I had been there just over two years and things were slowly moving forward. Our group was reaching out to other students, most who had little or no spiritual background. I love seeing students' lives being changed.

And our group began experiencing change..., only not the change I had hoped for.

New students were coming each week. But rather than seeing their lives changed, I was watching the lives of our own students being changed for the worse. Rather than influencing, they were being influenced.

I was discouraged, feeling literally exhausted. I arrived home after a student meeting you would like to forget, the kind of gathering that makes you wonder why you are even in ministry.

As we settled in for the night, I was in bed reading the Bible. That's when it occurred. That's when the words literally began leaping from the page. As I read the passage, it was strange, a good strange. God was literally speaking to me through the verses. It was as if God was saying, "Mark! Do you see this? Do you see what's happening? This is happening where you are right now. Listen up!"

For the next few minutes everything around me grew quiet.

I was reading about God speaking to Moses, preparing His people to enter into the Promised Land. More than 400 years earlier, God revealed His plan to Abram. Now under Moses' leadership, His plans were about to be fulfilled.

The Lord spoke to Moses.

"I will send my terror ahead of you and throw into confusion every nation you encounter. I will make all your enemies turn their backs and run. I will send the hornet ahead of you to drive the Hivites, Canaanites and Hittites out of your way."

And here is where things became very interesting.

"But I will not drive them out in a single year, because the land would become desolate and the wild animals too numerous for you. Little by little I will drive them out before you, until you have increased enough to take possession of the land (Exodus 23:27-30)."

Not in a single year? No immediate victory?

You will do things little by little, not all at once?

Why? Why make them wait?

It was because God loved them. The land was too immense for the people to handle. They were not yet strong enough, numerous enough to possess the land. They needed time to increase.

And that's where I was. That's where our ministry was. Our hearts were in the right place. We wanted to make a difference. But our maturity didn't match the mission. In short, we needed to grow up.

———————

God has blessed Carrie and me with five children. I am amazed by how much stuff seven people can accumulate over time. At least twice a year Carrie goes through all the kids' clothes, bags them by size and gives them to individuals or charities. I am embarrassed by the number of clothes we have.

It's not that we are greedy or selfish. In fact, many of the clothes we keep in tubs or totes, because they no longer fit. They are in great shape so we save them for the next kid in line. They are affectionately known as hand-me-downs. So we keep them and give the younger children time to grow.

———————

I really wanted to reach more students for Christ. But the hard truth was that our youth needed time to grow. So for the next six months, we took a different track.

I recruited a really sharp leader from within the church, divided our group in halves, and began a twenty-four week process of discipleship. It wasn't popular at first. We focused on the basics of our faith. We memorized Scripture. We prayed. We taught students the importance of daily reading God's Word, writing in a journal and recording the things they were learning. We had daily assignments and expected students to come each week having completed their work.

The group dwindled in numbers a bit, but I was convinced we were doing the right thing. It was little by little.

The last several months we placed our knowledge into action. Students began praying for their list of classmates and one by one, little by little, they shared Jesus with them. The students, not the leaders, shared their faith with friends.

It worked! It took time, but it worked.

The entire focus of our students changed. They not only wanted to make a difference in peoples' lives, they were prepared to make a difference in peoples' lives. And for me, student ministry was becoming fun again.

Within the next year, students were asking if they could meet and pray before school. I would pick up students at their houses beginning at 6 am on Fridays, where we would pray, read Scripture, and eat doughnuts before going to school.

Many of these students are still serving the Lord in a variety of ways. Some are stay-at-home moms, others are school teachers. One is a US Army Chaplain, another is an overseas missionary. Some struggled after graduation while others marched onward and advanced. And as I look back over those years of student ministry, this is the greatest reward of all.

———————

"Little by little" isn't a favorite phrase for most. It's difficult to wait. We don't want to wait. We want drive-thru experiences with immediate gratification. We want an Oompa Loompa and we want an Oompa Loompa now!

None of this should have hit me by surprise. Our students were not the only ones in need of growth. If I had paid more attention to the Gospels, I would have seen Jesus adopting the same strategy.

His public ministry lasted approximately 3 ½ years, beginning with His baptism by John and ending with His death, burial and resurrection. He knew His destiny. He understood the timing. He never seemed to hurry, content to walk with the Father.

While Jesus ministered to the crowds, His focus was always with a few. He wasn't taken in with the idea of a huge following. Instead He poured His life into twelve individuals. He traveled with them, taught them, corrected them, but most of all He loved them.

He modeled what ministry was all about – teaching others to teach others who might teach others. And He gave them time to grow, time to mature. And over the years, these ordinary and for the most part, uneducated men, were changed through time spent with Jesus.

That was His plan. He had no other. There was no back-up, no plan B.

Following His resurrection, Jesus ascended to heaven, placing the mission into the hands of a few. He passed the baton to those He had trained, little by little. He also gave them the gift of the Spirit, supplying them with power to accomplish the task at hand. They had everything they needed. We've been given all that is needed. "His divine power has given us everything we need for life and godliness (2 Peter 1:3)."

Jesus started with 12 which soon multiplied ten times. With the coming of the Holy Spirit, 3000 were soon added to that number in one day and daily, the Lord added to their number those being saved (Acts 2). Lives were transformed by the power of the Lord, by the power of His Holy Spirit. And within the disciples' lifetime, they had shared this message with their entire known world, without cell phones, internet, airplanes or cars. Little by little, they turned the world upside-down for Christ.

And little by little He will drive the enemy out before you, until you have increased enough to take possession of the land.

IT'S NOT COMPLICATED

⌁

"I don't have a whole lot of time. Can you just tell me how to get saved?"

Her name was Rachael. As a young high school student, she came to our Wednesday night youth worship service, the highlight of my week.

Students, along with their friends, would come each week. You never knew who might show. I taught our students that their school was the mission field. And while God may call some of them to serve in foreign countries one day, He was calling all of them to serve where they were that day.

They understood the concept.

Wednesday nights were fun, yet powerful. We would play some games or have a little friendly competition. Then we would sing songs or maybe watch a music video. Everything had a purpose and moved us toward the intended target.

Then I would take 20 minutes and teach from the Bible. Students would be given the opportunity to receive

Christ as Savior or ask questions about becoming a Christ-follower.

Rachel had questions.

"Could we talk?" she asked. "I want to know how to be saved."

So for the next 10 minutes we talked together in a corner of the room, while other students and leaders were hanging out. I shared with her the basics of becoming a believer.

God wants us to live with Him forever in heaven.

The problem is that God is perfect and we're not. We've all sinned and our sin separates us from God.

But God made a provision for our sin. Jesus came to earth, lived a sinless life, and willingly offered His life on a cross, making payment for our sin.

Rachael began looking at her watch.

Now that bothered me. Here I was speaking to Rachael about the most important decision of her life, and she was looking at her watch! I thought she was losing interest.

"Rachael," I asked. "Do you understand what I'm talking about here? Does all this so far make sense to you?"

"Yeah," she said. "I understand what you're saying."

"Rachael, this is the most important decision you will ever make in life. Why do you keep looking at your watch?"

"Well, my mother will be here to pick me up any minute. I don't have a whole lot of time. Can you just tell me how to get saved?"

We prayed.

Rachael asked the Lord's forgiveness and surrendered her life to Jesus as Savior and Lord. She had the widest smile on her face.

She then went outside, got into her mother's car, and went home a different person.

It's not complicated.

Why do we always make things so complicated?

———————

Complicated (com-pli-cat-ed): *Difficult to analyze, understand or explain; having many parts or steps.*[3]

Carrie believes baseball is a complicated sport. There are many rules to be sure. A great coach knows the rules and works within the rules to put his team in the best position to win. But in the end it's a simple game of pitch and catch, hit and run. You can't score runs without base runners. Get on base, however you can, and score more runs than the other team. The team with the most runs wins the game.

Marriage can be complicated. Will husbands ever really understand their wives and will wives truly understand their husbands? How much does that matter? It all boils down to love and commitment. I love you regardless and I'm committed to you.

At Mount Sinai, the Lord gave Moses ten commandments for living. They were basic commands about staying in right relation with God and man. Don't steal. Don't kill. Don't commit adultery. Honor your mother and father.

The fourth command was to remember the Sabbath and keep it holy. You have six days to work, so rest on the seventh.

But when Jesus came to earth He was accused of breaking His own laws. He healed people on the Sabbath, something the religious leaders had decided was work. No one was to work on the Sabbath. Their rules rose above relationships. They missed the forest for the trees. And their complicated system of beliefs was more than people could bear.

This is one reason people were attracted to Jesus. His message, for the most part was simple.

"Come follow me, and I will make you fishers of men (Matthew 4:19)."

"The work of God is this: to believe in the one he has sent (John 6:29)."

"I tell you the truth, he who believes has everlasting life (John 6:47)."

His teachings were such that people could understand.

A farmer went out to sow his seed.

Two men built a house, one on rock, one on sand.

A shepherd lost a sheep. A woman lost a coin. A father lost his son.

The Bible is an amazing book, written by men under the inspiration of God's Spirit. It is truth without error. And every day I read from it, I learn something new, something more. Yet at the core, the Bible teaches a simple, consistent message: God invites all people to a relationship with Him through faith in His Son Jesus. Repent and believe in the Lord Jesus and you will be saved.

The Pharisees in Jesus' day – the same guys upset with Him for healing a man on the Sabbath – tested Jesus by asking which of the commands was greatest. It had been determined there were 613 commands – 248 things you should do and 365 things you shouldn't. Talk about complicated. They were asking for simplicity.

"If you could boil it down to one thing, what would it be?"

To which Jesus replied (and I paraphrase), "Love the Lord your God with all you have. This is first and greatest. And the second is like it: Love your neighbor as yourself. Everything hangs from these two commands. (Matthew 22:37-40)."

Love God. Love others. It's not complicated.

I am convinced people are searching for simplicity, yearning for clarity. I am certain that many want to de-clutter their lives. At the heart of every human being lies the burning question, "What is my purpose? Why am I here? Does it all have to be so complicated?"

And the answer is very simply, no.

———————

One day as I was driving, I listened to a message by the late Adrian Rogers (I don't listen to many guys preach. I don't like to hear myself preach. I fear both are mistakes). He spoke about a man who had given him this advice, some of the best advice he had ever received. The man told Dr. Rogers he had learned, "One big decision will take care of many little decisions."

Following Jesus is a big decision. When a person surrenders his life to Jesus as Lord, he is literally handing over the reins, relinquishing control of his life. The apostle Paul wrote, "You are not your own; you were bought at a price (1 Corinthians 6:19-20)."

To lose your life to another is a major choice. But among other things, it is a choice that brings simplicity. Since I have decided to be who He wants me to be and do what He wants me to do, all that matters is pleasing Him. Is this pleasing to God? Is this in line with the Bible? If yes, move forward.

It's not complicated.

Another Rogers has influenced me – Mr. Rogers. I grew up watching Mr. Rogers' Neighborhood on PBS. Even as a kid, I knew something about the show was different. His show wasn't like other shows. It didn't "wow" me. It didn't have exciting plots or nail-biting action. Yet like millions of other kids, I was drawn to the show, drawn to the things Mr. Rogers taught.

Fred Rogers was an educator, minister, author and songwriter. In a documentary about his life, Mr. Rogers said two things that struck me most profoundly:

"Deep and simple is far more essential than shallow and complex."

"Simple is not the same as easy. Simple is often very difficult. Simple is right."[4]

I think Mr. Rogers listened to Jesus.

I HAD A DREAM

God speaks to His followers.

I hear a lot of people talk about how God said this and God said that. And while I know that God speaks to His people, I am not sure it's something we should talk about so lightly.

God does speak to people. Jesus said as much. "My sheep listen to my voice; I know them, and they follow me (John 10:27)."

God speaks to us primarily through the Bible. It's His Word. Most of what we need to know He has revealed to us through the Scriptures. That's why you need to spend time in the Bible, so you can know God more and better understand His will.

But God also speaks to us through prayer, other people and even circumstances. The way I figure, God can choose to speak to us by the Holy Spirit, in any way He chooses.

A few years out of seminary, I was part of a group studying Henry Blackaby's book Experiencing God. To this date, it is the best study I have ever undertaken. Experiencing God is about knowing and doing the will of God and looks at the different ways people in the Scriptures encountered God. I think Henry Blackaby has influenced a lot of people.

I was in the middle of this study when I had an incredible encounter with God. God spoke and I didn't take it lightly. It was what some call a spiritual marker, a defining moment, an asterisk on the page of life.

In sports, we call them game-changers. You play four quarters and still the final outcome hinges on one or two plays – game changers.

My game-changer occurred one day during the early morning hours. I was asleep; fast asleep.

I had this dream.

I was knee-deep in the middle of a clear, cold fast running river. Each summer my family would spend one week in Texas hill country where we would swim, float and fish along the Frio River. It was this river.

I stood there alone in the river, holding only a match. I heard God say, "Strike the match under the water."

"Strike the match under water? Lord, I can't do that," I protested.

Once more the Lord said, "Strike the match underwater."

"But Lord," I said. "I can't do that. It's impossible."

And God said, "That's right. You can't do it. But I can. And there are things I am going to do through you that only I can do."

With that I woke up. I was shaken.

I rolled over and said to Carrie, "Get up. I need to tell you something."

I recalled the dream with my wife. I also wrote the entire event down in a journal so I could go back and revisit the moment.

I feel the need to say something here. I have dreamed a lot of weird things in my life. I have dreamed things that I would be ashamed to put down in print. Some nights I will wake up after a strange dream and think *how could I ever come up with something like that?*

That's the truth.

I have a lot of dreams, and most of them don't seem to be from God. But not this one. Without question, this one was from God.

My mind was spinning. *What does God have in store? What are His plans? Wow! God actually wants to work through me so much that He even told me in a dream!*

The next day, God spoke again. This time, He spoke through the Scriptures.

I was reading about the calling of the prophet Elisha.

The current prophet, Eli-JAH, was preparing to pass his mantle to Eli-SHA. Elisha would be his successor.

Elisha was a farmer. When the two meet, Elisha is plowing his fields with a team of oxen. Elijah places his cloak around him, symbolic of his new calling. Elisha leaves the oxen and announces that he needs to tell his parents good-bye (seems logical to me).

Elijah, upon hearing the announcement, tells him to go back.

Realizing what he has done, Elisha slaughters his oxen, breaks the plows into firewood, and cooks filet mignon for the entire community.

He burns every bridge. If ever tempted to return to his old ways, there would be nothing of which to return.

At that moment, I sensed God saying to me, "When I call, be ready to leave."

While my dream the previous morning had shaken me, my afternoon experience in God's Word seemed just as powerful. I knew God was speaking to me. I recognized His voice.

The next day, God spoke to me through an experience. I have been taught, and strongly believe, we need to be very careful interpreting our experiences. Experiences can lie. We can read things into them that are not there. I'm pretty sure Henry Blackaby taught me that as well.

It was early the next morning. I rose out of my sleep to hit the snooze button on my alarm, one second before the alarm went off. I turned off the alarm as it was about to ring.

I lay down in my bed, chuckled to myself and said, "Boy, that was good timing."

Just then, the Spirit of God said, "Trust Me. My timing is perfect."

And once more, I knew exactly what God was saying.

After this, God was silent. I continued to read the Bible. I prayed each morning. I spent time alone with God most every day. But I heard nothing new.

I am going to do things through you that only I can do. When I call you to them, be ready to follow.

Trust Me. My timing is perfect.

I felt sort of like Indiana Jones, searching for hidden treasure. Life was an adventure. What was God going to do? What does He have in store?

For the next several months, God began revealing to me, that I would pastor a church. I was a youth pastor at the time and loved what I was doing. I would often tell people that while I may not be a youth pastor all my life, one thing was certain, I would never pastor a church.

Don't you love it when you tell God your plans?

Over the next several months, God took the very thing that I never wanted to be, and made it the very thing I desired. His desire became my desire.

I saw a church in the neighboring city was looking for a pastor. I felt drawn to the church and submitted a resume. I would drive to the church, stop in the parking lot, and pray. I remember one time literally weeping over that church.

It's hard to explain, but somehow I knew God was going to send me to there. And He did. God gave me the pleasure of pastoring a wonderful group of people who love God and love others. They weren't perfect, but neither was I.

One year from the day God first told me to strike a match under the cold Frio River, I was voted in as pastor of the church. One year. God used that time period to shape me and prepare me for the task at hand.

You might be wondering, "Did God ever do those great things through you that only He could do? What has He done? Did you build a big church? Witness great miracles?"

Truthfully, I often go back to that experience and ask myself the same question. "God, what have you done here that others contribute to You? What has happened at this church that causes people to say, 'This could ONLY be the work of God'?"

And better yet, "Lord, what do you still have in store that only You can do?"

I'm still living the dream literally – serving, listening, watching, and waiting.

I have seen God do things that only He can do. People have trusted Christ as Savior. Lives have been changed. People have been healed. I have been blessed to see the hand of God in numerous ways. But I confess I'm not satisfied.

Don't get me wrong. I am content, just not satisfied.

Part of it might be this whole numbers-driven, success-oriented mindset we have of the church. You know, "How many did you have in church last Sunday? Is your church growing?" Stuff like that.

And that's all good. I really do want the church to reach more and more people. I want to see more people come to know the Lord personally. I really do. I want to be with more people in heaven and create a better place here on earth in the meanwhile.

But I'm still searching. I'm still praying. I'm still dreaming. I still have a dream.

If a kitchen match is going to strike underwater, it will happen only because God causes it to happen. By natural law it's impossible. With man's ability, it can never happen.

So here is the question I'm asking myself, a question we all need to answer: "What am I attempting in life right now that will only occur if God intervenes? What have I ever attempted that would cause me to fall flat on my face, unless God stepped in? When was the last time I truly risked anything for God?"

I believe the most common answer might be *nothing or never.* I hope I'm wrong. It is just that we usually say we are attempting something only God could do, while in truth we have a back-up plan in case He doesn't come through. Most of what we attempt, we can do in our abilities. We talk like we're striking matches underwater but in truth we are high and dry far above the surface.

I want to see a match light underwater. I want to strike a match in the deep.

I DO AND I DID

Our family was getting larger, so we decided to buy a

It all started with a flock of seagulls.

Our family was getting larger, so we decided to buy a bigger, older home in our city. The house was located on a street running toward the bay. We were only 400 yards from the water.

We loved that house.

We had great neighbors. There was a constant breeze. There were always birds flying, particularly seagulls.

Our son always loved chasing birds from the front yard. Wearing only a diaper, he would run full-speed at the gulls, yelling as he went, literally chasing them from the yard. It was loads of entertainment for us all.

One day I was home watching the kids and cooking dinner when the phone rang. I was doing what parents do best – multitasking. I was talking, stirring, baking and watching kids, only now I didn't see all the kids.

Where was my son? He was there a few minutes ago.

"Hold on just a minute," I told my friend on the phone. "Let me check on the kids."

I checked the bedroom but he wasn't in his bedroom.

I searched the house, but came up empty.

"He must be outside," I told myself. I looked in the backyard and then in the front. My two-year old son was nowhere to be found.

"I will call you back. I have to go," I told my friend.

It was the moment many parents have when they can't find their child. He's often in the clothes rack of the store, or on the candy aisle at the grocery. Usually everything is okay, usually. But in this particular moment, everything was not okay.

His brother and I began to look. We searched all the places we had searched before. Maybe he was hiding or playing a game. Maybe he fell asleep. We looked in all the rooms, all the closets, backyard and front yard.

And then I saw him. He was four houses down chasing seagulls from the neighbor's yard. He nearly made it to the end of our street!

It was decision-time. Do I hug him because I found him, or discipline him for running away? Yes.

"Son, you can't run down the street like that chasing birds. You could get hurt. You could get lost. You can't leave this yard unless Daddy is outside with you!"

"Yeah," his five-year-old brother chimed in. "You're going to get in trouble. Wait until Momma comes home!"

It got very quiet.

"No son," I said. "We don't want to tell Momma. It might upset her. Let's just keep this between us guys."

And we did.

Several days later I was at the office when the phone rang. It was my wife.

"Mark," she said. "You're not going to believe this. Today I was cleaning house and got busy doing a bunch of things. I started looking for the kids and I couldn't find our son. I looked everywhere and started to panic.

"You are never going to believe where he was."

"Where," I asked?

"He was three doors down in the neighbor's yard chasing birds! The Fed-Ex guy had stopped his truck to check on him."

That's when I replied, "Honey, how could you do that? How could you let our son get out of your sight so quickly! That could be dangerous."

Not really. I didn't say that..., really.

To the woman I once said, "I do", I confessed, "I did."

"I didn't tell you this, but the same thing happened to me just the other day."

Then I recounted my story to her.

"We need to do something about this to make sure it doesn't happen again."

We did. And fortunately it never happened again.

You see, as a parent I blew it. All parents blow it from time to time. But I didn't want my wife to know. I didn't want anyone to know.

It wasn't until Carrie admitted her mistake that I was willing to admit mine. It often works that way, particularly at church.

I don't know why, but for several weeks there seemed to be an imaginary "Hit Me" sign on the back of our suburban. Our car was hit three times in three weeks – once while moving, once while stopped and another when parked. It was a giant magnet attracting the worst of drivers.

Yet few people ever knew. There were dings and dents, even a bumper that needed replacement. But I have this friend Augie. He works at a body shop.

They pull out the dents, straighten the bumps and replace broken parts. Then they sand it down smoothly and feather in matching paint. Those guys are really good.

Before you knew it, we were back on the road, looking good as new. As I pulled into the church parking lot, no one was aware we had been hit, bruised, bumped or damaged.

We all come to church
And soon take our places.
We smile at each other,
With bright shiny faces.

Why do we feel so compelled to hide our imperfections?

———

Some are afraid of being judged or condemned. "If I admit this awful habit or struggle in my life, what will people think of me? If I'm transparent, people might know I don't have it all together."

In truth, some of you have been condemned by others. You were honest and you were burned. So you have raised the drawbridge and stood guard at your castle.

The irony is everyone already knows you don't have it all together, because they don't have it all together. None of us have it all together. So can we all quit acting like we have it all together?

We need to be authentic. We need to be real, transparent, genuine individuals. There is no need to air our dirty laundry at inappropriate times. But we need to quit acting like we have it all together when in fact, we don't.

Coming together corporately as followers of Christ is about confessing to God we don't have it all together. If we could save ourselves there would be no need for the Savior we worship.

In order for us to lower our bridges we need safety, love, and acceptance. We don't need to erase our moral standards, or compromise biblical truth. Speak the truth, but speak the truth in love. Love one another.

The truth is we all fall short. We have all been bruised. We've all sinned.

He doesn't just pick you up, pull out the dents and give you a new outer coating. He makes you brand new. He makes you what the Bible calls, a new creation – a truth which isn't for the birds.

ARE YOU HAVING FUN YET?

[decorative flourish]

"What's cooking, dude. Are you having fun, yet?"

Those were pretty much his first words to me.

I was in my office working on Sunday's message when this big guy knocked, stood in my open doorway, and asked me if I was having fun. His name was Walter, Brother Walter to most.

He was the new pastor in a neighboring community. He was driving back from visiting someone in the hospital and stopped by to say hey. I knew right away this man was different. I knew right away I was going to like him.

Most people when they first talk to a pastor, especially if it's another pastor, ask how things are going in the church. "How big is your church? Is it growing? How many are in your congregation?"

They are well-intentioned mostly. I just don't think they know what else to ask. Or maybe that's what our American culture has conditioned people to ask?

But Walter never asked me that question..., ever. He probably knew I'd lie and make up some impressive story. Or maybe he knew there were more important questions to ask.

"Are you having fun? What's God doing in your life? Tell me something you've learned in the last few weeks. Let's go eat."

It was refreshing to say the least.

Walter was more than ten years my elder. I was still somewhat new to ministry, while he had some pastoral experience. And for the next several years, I learned as much as I could from the man.

"Who you are is more important than what you do."

If I heard it once from Walter, I heard it a hundred times. If I have said it once, I have said it two hundred times.

We are always focused on what we do. Let's face it. American culture defines us by two criteria: (1) what you have and (2) what you do.

This is why I think Walter would never ask me how big the church was getting. Life is not about what you have. Life is about who you are. It's about being, not about doing. You are a human being, not a human doing.

Some of you might disagree at this point. I understand the Bible says it's important that we do the right things. For example, James tells us in the Bible not simply to hear the Word of God but to do what it says. Jesus said, "Whoever hears His words and puts them into practice is like a wise man who builds his house upon the rock (Matthew 7:24)."

Doing is important, but never more important than being. You could do all the right things, have a great outward appearance, but inwardly your heart could still be dark. Jesus said a lot about that as well.

But the big reason being is more important than doing, according to Walter, is...

> "Changing what you do never changes who
> you are. But when Jesus changes who you
> are, this always changes what you do."

God works from the inside out, and for some reason we always think outside in. It's the best we can do really. We can only change what we do in hopes it will change who we are. But changing what we do never changes who we are.

We know that by experience. If I were this terrible man who built houses for a living and one day decided to become a dentist, I would still be a terrible man. The only difference is I would pull teeth instead of permits. Outwardly I would still be the same guy.

If I wanted to become a more proficient writer, I might take classes or read books. And though as a result I may publish greater works and influence more readers, my character, or lack thereof, remains untouched. I have changed only what I do and that never changes who I am.

So how can I change who I am?

I can't. But God can. He is the catalyst, the agent of change.

I received Christ as Savior at age 9. He came to live within me in the person of the Holy Spirit. The Holy Spirit took up residence in me and the process of change began. I was, as the Bible says, born again.

Sometimes the change is drastic. Other times I feel as though He is just chipping away.

Some changes come quickly at microwave-speed. Others stew slowly in the crock pot.

But there is change. There is always change. You must have change. Like a coke machine out of quarters, you must have correct change.

And that correct change is evidence of the Holy Spirit in my life. He changed who I am and that has changed what I have done.

———————

The Bible tells about a man who approached Jesus one day. He was young. He was wealthy and he was searching. Though he was successful in every sense of our world's definition, something was missing.

I am certain he had heard Jesus teach. No doubt he had witnessed Jesus helping or healing others. He was impressed by what he had seen, what he had heard about the Christ. So he took what was his greatest question to the greatest teacher. "Teacher, what good thing must I do to get eternal life (Matthew 19:16)?"

Did you catch that? Read his question once again. "What good thing must I DO to get eternal life?" Likely, everything to this point in his life had been earned. He worked hard to attain his status.

Jesus replied, "If you want to enter life, obey the commandments. Do not murder, do not commit adultery, do not steal, do not give false testimony, honor your father and mother, and love your neighbor as yourself (Matthew 19:17, 18)."

"All these I have kept," the young man said. "What do I still lack (Verse 20)?"

He was no heathen looking for help. He wasn't this terrible man with a terrible past. Here was a fine, upstanding Jewish young man. He knew the commands of God. He kept the commands of God. Yet, inside he still lacked something. There was a still a hole in his soul that couldn't be filled by doing.

"Jesus answered, 'If you want to be perfect, go sell your possessions and give to the poor, and you will have treasure in heaven. Then come, follow me.' (Verse 21)"

"When the young man heard this, he went away sad, because he had great wealth (Verse 22)."

He had worked hard. He had done much. And now Jesus was telling him to surrender all of his doing in exchange for being.

He couldn't do it. He couldn't muster the courage. He couldn't turn loose of that which defined him, and he went away sad.

The disciples could hardly believe their eyes. For one, they believed if a man was rich, certainly it was because of God's favor, God's blessing. To them, material wealth was a tell-tale sign that God was on your side. That's why they were stunned by Jesus next statement. "How hard it is for the rich to enter the kingdom of God (Mark 10:23)."

And secondly, they lost a great prospect, a potential team member. Here was a man that was wealthy, influential and interested in Jesus. And within a few short statements, Jesus let him slip right through his fingers.

"Jesus looked at him and loved him (Verse 21)."

Matthew had left his tax collecting profession. James and John abandoned the family fishing business. They had left all to follow Jesus, but not this man. He held on to his wealth while his wealth held onto him. He had all that he needed and nothing he wanted.

Like the man who walked into my office one day declaring, "I'm not yet 40 years old. I have a successful practice. I own my home and cars. I have no debt. And I'm miserable." Fortunately he is now learning that life is about being, not doing or even having.

I learned all I could from Walter. He retired early due to health reasons. A few years following retirement, he passed away.

But like any good mentor, his teachings outlived his life on earth. That's the purpose of mentoring – to multiply ourselves. We are to teach others what we've been taught, in hopes they will teach others to teach others.

And one day soon I may come knocking on your office door asking, *"Are you having fun, yet?"*

HOLD ON!

My family enjoys the outdoors.

We love to swim and fish and go to the beach. We also like to hunt.

Not everyone enjoys hunting. I understand. But some of my favorite times growing up were spent hunting in the brush country of South Texas with my father. I have been blessed to have the same experiences with my children, especially the boys.

I first began taking them when they turned age 6. I take the boys to the family ranch where we basically rough it for two to three days. It is not without challenge.

You see, when you go hunting, you have to be quiet. If you are not quiet, you don't see any animals. When your son is young, you don't see many animals.

It's hard for a little boy to stay quiet. He has lots of questions. He points at everything he sees. If he doesn't see anything after a few minutes, he is ready to leave.

I usually carry snacks to eat. You can't take too many drinks or that leads to another problem when hunting.

It was mid-afternoon when my six-year-old son and I left the cabin to hunt. It was a cold afternoon. I bundled him up in his camouflage pants and coat. He had an orange wool cap pulled over his ears.

A walk is always good on a cold day. It keeps you warm as you work up a sweat.

We hadn't been walking long when my son started talking. Now remember, you have to stay quiet if you are going to see any animals. We hadn't arrived at our hunting location yet and he was already talking!

I tried to ignore him. I certainly wasn't going to carry on a conversation. So I kept hold of his hand and continued to walk.

He kept saying the same thing over and again. I couldn't quite make out his words. They weren't making sense. I kept walking.

"I got no I. I got no I," he said.

"I got no I, daddy. I got no I."

"I got no I?" I thought. "What do you mean I got no I?"

Finally, I looked down at my young son to see that his orange wool cap had slipped down on his head, below his nose and was covering both eyes.

For the first time I understood, "I got no eye!"

He couldn't see!

I felt horrible. Okay, I actually laughed but I did feel sort of bad.

But then another thought occurred. For the last 100 yards my son couldn't see but he continued to walk. And the only reason he continued to walk was the grip he held on his daddy's hand. He wasn't walking by sight.

———

If you are a follower of Jesus, your entire life is a journey of faith – a faith walk, if you will. We enter a relationship with the Father through faith in Jesus. We are called to live each day by faith in Him. Without faith, the Bible says, it's impossible to please God.

From beginning to end, our lives are marked by faith. Sometimes I demonstrate a lot of faith, while other times my faith is sorely lacking. I thank God that when I am at times faithless, He remains faithful.

The New Testament book of Hebrews devotes an entire chapter to men and women of the Old Testament that demonstrated great faith. Hebrews chapter 11 says that "faith is being sure of what we hope for and certain of what we do not see." The writer then goes on to describe people like Abel and Enoch, Noah and Abraham, Isaac, Joseph, and Moses. The list continues mentioning Rahab, Gideon, Samson, and David.

At first you might think this is a list of superheroes like Batman, Superman, and Wonder Woman. And indeed they showed near superhero faith. But in truth, they were people in many ways just like you, just like me. They were said to be people "whose weakness was turned to strength (Hebrews 11:34)."

They couldn't always see where they were going. They didn't initially have all the answers. Abraham went to a land that God would show him. Noah had never seen rain. Moses tried convincing God he wasn't the man for the job.

But somehow they held on to the Father's hand.

We often want to see the details before following God. God wants us to follow Him so He can show us the details. We want to walk by sight. God wants us walking in faith. We want to see to believe. He wants belief so we might see.

———

Once when I was praying, I felt God wanted me to give $100 to a friend's ministry. I had the money but things were tight. I told myself I would mail a check, but didn't do it right away. I delayed.

The next day I went to the mailbox and there was a letter with a check made to me for $100. I immediately wrote my friend a check for $100 and placed it in the mail.

While I made good on my promise to give the money, I missed the opportunity given me by God. I had a chance to give in faith and instead I gave by sight.

———

Not long after coming to our church as pastor, I remember walking down the church hallway, realizing something wasn't right. I was walking downhill.

A week or so later, I began noticing a crack in the wall and a crack in the floor. There were issues with the building's foundation.

A reputable company came and inspected our building. We needed our foundation re-leveled to the tune of $10,000. This may or may not seem like a great sum of money to you, but to our small congregation, it was a chunk of change.

The church was still recovering from a rock-bottom economy and had significant debt from a previous building. Yet, we had to address the situation soon or things would only grow worse and costs would simply increase.

So we arranged for repairs and set the date. In six weeks the company would come and begin their work. Some way, somehow we would have the money.

People sacrificed. People gave. Little by little money came in. We created a visual for the church foyer. Every week you could see the progress we were making.

We put the information in our monthly newsletter mailed to a number of people. We would often get checks from past and present members. Each week was like Christmas as we opened the mail to see what might come.

Finally, it was time to begin. The company would begin its work on Tuesday. After receiving offerings on Sunday, we were only $300 short of our goal.

I walked into the church office on Tuesday morning. Our Administrative Assistant arrived at the same time, carrying mail she picked up from the Post Office. Before going through the stack of letters I said, "Let's look through the mail and find our missing $300."

We laughed together as she sorted through papers. There was a personal letter among the pile, hand-addressed to the church. I sat down, said a prayer, and opened the envelope.

"We read about the needed repairs for the church foundation. We are former members of the church and loved our time spent there. After moving to Houston we joined another church but are currently looking for another place to serve. During this interim, we wanted to send our tithe back to Oak Ridge."

Enclosed were two checks totaling...$300.

God tested our faith and we had passed.

———————

I take the same test often. It's always a pass or fail exam. Some tests are harder than others. Some are simple, others more difficult.

But that's what life with Christ is all about – walking in faith. We bring honor to Him as we walk together in faith.

Take hold of your Father's hand and walk.

PAIN

⌒♏︎⌒

As the parents of five children, we are on a first name basis with our doctor and have the local hospital on speed dial. There is no way to recall all our trips to the ER.

There have been stitches to the mouth, a broken arm, stitches to the head, dehydration, stitches to the eye, RSV, stitches to the leg and a fish hook through the arm. And these are but a few.

I may be wrong, but I don't think it is all that unusual. I mean, if you have children, you're going to have bumps and bruises. And while we do our best to protect the kids, life happens.

But of all our medical encounters, one stands apart from the rest.

At age five, our oldest daughter Caroline kept having fever. It would come and go. Each time she contracted a fever, we would give her some meds and soon everything was fine. But within a few days it would come back again. She just couldn't seem to shake it.

I'm always the one who thinks everything is going to be okay. Carrie on the other hand, isn't quick to let things go. She knew something wasn't right.

We were getting ready for bed one evening, when our daughter woke up crying. Her leg was hurting. Her right leg was hurting.

She is a tall girl. I assumed she was having growing pains. That's because I think everything is always all right. The next day we were at the doctor's office.

We explained everything to the doctor. He listened thoroughly. We are blessed with a great pediatrician.

"I going to schedule an MRI," he said.

We went to the local children's hospital that day, the same hospital we have on speed dial.

The radiologist told us our daughter had an infection, a bone infection. Somehow, some germ made it through her skin, into her bloodstream and settled in her hip. It was literally eating away bone in her hip.

She went straight to a room and the next day a line was surgically implanted into an artery. For the next three months my wife and I administered IV antibiotics three times a day through the line. In the end, her body was clear of all infection. We thank God.

We also thanked our pediatrician for his quick and accurate diagnosis. He caught the infection at an early stage.

"You know, Mark," he said. "You were very fortunate. Once the infection entered her bloodstream, it could have settled nearly anywhere in her body. But because it settled in her hip, she experienced pain while walking and running. That enabled us to detect it early and prevent more extensive damage."

Her pain was a tool used by God that literally saved her leg and perhaps her life.

———————

Professor Pain is a difficult teacher, isn't he?

I don't always like him. In fact, at first I never like him. I want to drop his class. Pain hurts. Pain is hard to take. But few things teach as well as pain.

I have walked the winning run across home plate.

I missed a ground ball allowing the winning run to score.

I was dumped by my high school sweet heart two months into college.

I nearly quit seminary trying to figure out which way was up.

Together my wife and I have experienced miscarriage.

I have buried family members, friends, teenagers and children.

I have had people leave the church after serving together for years.

That's just some of my list. I am sure you have your own. Pain is no respecter of persons. In fact, when I look at my life, the pains that I have endured nearly pale in comparison to what I have witnessed in others.

I'm careful when I talk to people about pain. There is a lot I don't understand about pain. Besides, when someone is experiencing pain, they are usually not looking for answers. There is no comfort in answers. So mostly I just listen.

I cause a lot of my pain. I think God causes some pain, but not all pain. One thing is for sure, He certainly allows it.

Like the pain in my daughter's leg. I was so grateful for that pain. And I am grateful for a lot of the pain I have experienced.

I have learned much through pain.

I have helped people through my pain.

I have matured as a follower of Christ because of my pain.

And then there is pain that seems to have no purpose at all; at least no purpose that I can see. That's the most difficult of pains to endure.

The Bible tells about a man named Jacob. His life story spans nearly 25 chapters of the book of Genesis. He was the son of Isaac and the grandson of Abraham.

The name Jacob means 'deceiver' and boy was he ever. He deceived his father. He deceived his brother. He deceived his father-in-law (though some may say he deserved it). And he deceived his brother still again.

I can remember the first time I studied the life of Jacob. The only thing good I could find was God's grace. If God could show grace to a deceiver like Jacob, then God could be gracious to me!

But Jacob was also determined. He was a fighter. And one night he fought with God.

During his match, the Bible says that "God touched the socket of Jacob's hip so that his hip was wrenched as he wrestled...and he was limping because of his hip."

The Lord said, "Your name will no longer be Jacob, but Israel, because you have struggled with God and with men and have overcome (see Genesis 32:22-32)."

Like my little Caroline, Jacob experienced pain in his hip. But unlike my daughter, his pain never left.

The writer of Hebrews, when describing men and women of faith, devotes one verse of Scripture to Jacob the deceiver; Jacob the overcomer.

"By faith Jacob, when he was dying, blessed each of Joseph's sons, and worshiped as he leaned on the top of his staff (Hebrews 11:21)."

Did you catch that? He worshiped as he leaned on the top of his staff.

It seems our brother Jacob walked in pain the rest of his life. God used his pain as a constant reminder of the strength and power of almighty God.

For in our weakness God is strong.

HOW DOES YOUR GARDEN GROW?

I have always enjoyed gardening with the kids. There is so much to learn. It teaches them to work. It teaches them to wait. It teaches responsibility. But more than anything, I love seeing the look on their faces when they first see fruit beginning to grow on plants they have placed into the ground.

We once had a garden to the side of our house. It wasn't very large, but you might be surprised at how much you can grow in small areas if your garden is well-designed.

This particular spot was great. It received shade in the morning and sun in the afternoon. There was a fence on one side that protected smaller plants from the gulf breezes of the Texas coast.

I had planned out the garden that particular year with squash, onions, peppers, radishes and large, beefy red tomatoes. Everything had its place. We went to the local nursery and selected our plants and seeds.

After hours of work everything was ready. All we needed were the three W's – watering, weeding and waiting.

I don't recall the plants every growing so quickly. They really took off. It was exciting. We watched the squash bloom and the radishes grow. We watered and fertilized religiously.

But more than anything, we were watching the tomatoes. We had selected a variety of large beefy red tomatoes. If there is anything you want to show off in your garden, it is the tomatoes. We actually have people in our church that will leave large baskets of tomatoes in the foyer free to anyone who wants them. I wanted to leave a basket of really large tomatoes in the church foyer.

The tomato plants grew tall. In fact, they grew very tall. I bought vegetable cages to place around the plants for support. The plants responded by growing even taller. And suddenly, as if overnight, the plants began to bloom.

There were lots of blooms. I'd never seen that many blooms. I began to wonder how one plant could support so many large beefy red tomatoes. I knew I had some special plants. I couldn't wait to leave that basket in the church foyer…, for those who needed tomatoes, of course.

Soon the blooms gave way to fruit. Small green balls began appearing everywhere. They began getting larger but suddenly stopped growing at the size of a grape. Then they turned red – ripe red.

I didn't have large beefy red tomatoes. I had what we call cherry tomatoes. Some call them grape tomatoes. I had gallons upon gallons of a small variety of tomatoes, great for salads, or home-made picante. They are the last thing you want to put in the church foyer. Some kid, somewhere, is still laughing about switching the labels on my tomato plants at the store.

And I was none the wiser, that is, until I saw the fruit. When the plants are young, they look the same. When the plants are still growing, there is little difference. Only by their fruits can they be distinguished.

I am a pastor, not a botanist. I can look at trees and have no idea whether they are orange trees, apple trees or lemon trees. To my untrained eye, they are simply trees. But when I see an apple on the end of the branch or a limb full of lemons, all bets are off. There is no denying the fruit.

Jesus said, "I am the vine; you are the branches. If a man remains in me and I in him, he will bear much fruit; apart from me you can do nothing (John 15:5)." He also said, "This is to my Father's glory, that you bear much fruit, showing yourselves to be my disciples (John 15:8)."

Like fruit on a tree, the fruit from our lives is a dead give-away. It shows who we are or who we are not. The outer fruit is evidence of the inner life. We show ourselves to be His disciples by bearing fruit that not only looks like the Lord but is actually of the Lord. It's what the Bible calls fruit of the Spirit.

Our lives should be a cornucopia of love, joy, peace, patience, kindness, goodness, faithfulness, gentleness and self-control (Galatians 5:22 – 23). These are the fruits of the Spirit. These are the characteristics of God.

The Holy Spirit comes to reside in the heart of the born-again follower of Christ. If you are born-again, you are indwelled by His Spirit. And the evidence of the Spirit, the evidence of a changed life, is the fruit of the Spirit.

I can't yield these traits myself. I can't somehow produce them by self-effort or religious fervor. They are not man-made, but rather Spirit-produced.

He is the vine. We are merely branches. The fruit is produced through the vine. The only job for the branch is to stay connected to the vine. If I will just stay connected, the fruit will come. "By their fruit," Jesus said, "you will recognize them (Matthew 7:16)."

———————

In His Parable of the Soils (Matthew 13 and Mark 4), Jesus tells the story of a farmer planting seeds. As the farmer scatters the seeds, they fall upon different soils. The seed is the truth of God's Word, the Good News of Jesus. The soil is the heart of man.

The seed is constant. It never changes. The soil, like the heart of man, varies.

Some hearts are hard like the path people travel. The seed cannot penetrate the path, so birds from above take the seed from the surface of the soil.

Others hearts are shallow like rocky places in the field. While the seed gets under the surface, the roots have no depth. There is very little soil in the rocks. As the sun rises, the plant is scorched and dies.

Some hearts are like soil infested with weeds. They are distracted by other pursuits and concerns. The weeds choke the plant and hold back the potential fruit.

But other hearts are prepared. They are ready to receive the truth. The seed is planted on good soil. Roots grow deep. A great harvest is produced.

You have witnessed them all. One of them is yours. One of them is mine. There are hardened hearts, shallow hearts, preoccupied hearts, and prepared hearts. But only one heart produces the fruit. Only the heart prepared to receive the truth of God experiences its created purpose of bearing fruit.

Go and bear fruit.

———————

One final story.

Some years back, Carrie and I were invited to spend a weekend in a home along the coast. We quickly accepted the invitation as time alone is always a premium.

It was a 90-minute drive to the bay house, which sat in a somewhat secluded area. Along the way, we drove through an area where family on my mother's side settled years ago. They were farmers.

And like many farming families of their day, they had lots of children. There were thirteen brothers and sisters. Their home was in the middle of nowhere and with the exception of trees throughout the yard they were surrounded by miles of fields and farmland. I had not seen the old homestead in many years.

As a kid, I remember visiting my great-grandparents at their farm on several occasions, most often on holidays. It was a big house filled with lots of kinfolk. I didn't like going there very much. It was loud. Everyone seemed to know me but I didn't know them. Besides, they always wanted me to sing or tell a joke. I remember sitting next to my bed-ridden great grandfather and talking and listening for what seemed like hours.

On our second day at the bay house, I decided to look for the old farm. I wanted to show it to Carrie so she could learn a bit more of my family's history.

As we drove down back roads with twists and turns, I was recounting to her stories of my childhood. I was telling her about this huge house filled with holiday memories. I recognized a few landmarks and knew I was in the right area.

And suddenly the road came to an end.

"That's odd," I told her. "I remembered the house sitting somewhere before this road came to an end."

We had passed the house.

I turned through the ditch and went back about 100 yards. There it was. I recognized the trees. But that couldn't be the house, could it?

It looked more like a shack, a run-down shack with a collapsed front porch. I sat there, staring at the house from the car window. Yet, the longer I looked I realized it was the house. It just looked so small and so old. It wasn't the house I remembered. But it was the house in which they once lived. And the days of her former glory had passed.

———

God doesn't want you stuck in the past. He has no desire for you to live constantly remembering the good old days. Learn from your past. Don't live there.

God calls each of us to a life-long journey with the Savior. If you are banking on some commitment you once made as a child, or a church experience back in grade school, you have missed the point.

He is not a drive-thru Jesus.

He isn't looking for you simply to pray a prayer so you can claim membership in His club. He wants to walk with you and He wants you to walk with Him.

He's looking for a sit-down dinner where He might fellowship with those who are His. He wants you to know Him at the deepest levels. He wants to teach you throughout all of life as He uses all things to shape you more and more into His image.

He wants us all to follow Him.

ENDNOTES

1   *Baseball Almanac*. Baseball-Almanac.com (accessed August 18, 2014).
2   Tozier, A.W. (2009). *The Knowledge of the Holy*. HarperOne.
3   *Merriam Webster Dictionary*. M-W.com (accessed June 2014).
4   Benjamin Wagner,"*46 Things I Learned Making Mr. Rogers and Me*". *(February 27, 2014): MentalFloss.com (accessed May 2014).*

CONNECT WITH MARK

One of the great lessons God continues to reinforce with me is the truth that He is taking everything in life and working it together for my good and His glory. He is teaching us daily in innumerable ways. Just look about you! See God in the everyday patterns and happenings of life.

If you would like to receive my free weekly devotion, purchase additional copies of this book, or simply connect on-line then visit...

www.inallyourways.com

"Trust in the Lord with all your heart and lean not on your own understanding; **in all your ways** acknowledge Him, and He will make your paths straight."

Proverbs 3:5 - 6

CPSIA information can be obtained at www.ICGtesting.com
Printed in the USA
LVOW07s0016181114

414222LV00001B/24/P